T0197193

Ego on Front Street

ALSO, BY ROBIN L. JOHNSON

Awakening of a Chocolate Mystic (Balboa Press 2011)

ETA 2 Oneness: A Journey to
Spiritual Awakening (Balboa Press 2014)

Ego on Front Street

ROBIN L. JOHNSON

BALBOA.PRESS
A DIVISION OF HAY HOUSE

Balboa Press books may be ordered through booksellers or by contacting:

Balboa Press
A Division of Hay House
1663 Liberty Drive
Bloomington, IN 47403
www.balboapress.com
844-682-1282

Because of the dynamic nature of the Internet, any web addresses or
links contained in this book may have changed since publication and
may no longer be valid. The views expressed in this work are solely those
of the author and do not necessarily reflect the views of the publisher,
and the publisher hereby disclaims any responsibility for them.

The author of this book does not dispense medical advice or prescribe
the use of any technique as a form of treatment for physical, emotional,
or medical problems without the advice of a physician, either directly
or indirectly. The intent of the author is only to offer information
of a general nature to help you in your quest for emotional and
spiritual well-being. In the event you use any of the information in
this book for yourself, which is your constitutional right, the author
and the publisher assume no responsibility for your actions.

The cover photo was taken in Cape Town, South
Africa by author Robin L. Johnson

Print information available on the last page.

ISBN: 979-8-7652-3537-9 (sc)
ISBN: 979-8-7652-3536-2 (e)

Library of Congress Control Number: 2022918773

Balboa Press rev. date: 11/02/2022

To my family and friends, thanks for helping me see myself clearly and for teaching me to "own my contribution to the chaos."

"The human ungoverned is more vicious than the animal in the jungle."
St. Germain

Contents

Foreword
By Shama Khurana
Spiritual Transformation Coach, United Kingdom

I am so honoured to be asked by Robin to write this foreword for her third book – "Ego on Front Street." I have found each of Robin's magnificent books so captivating as though the Divine were speaking directly to me through Robin's words. Robin's style of writing is so heartwarming, I found it impossible to put these books down.

When I saw the title of this book, Ego on Front Street, it made me stop in my tracks. What a title? What does this really mean, as I was not aware of this phrase? As always, when I started reading this latest book and without fail, I was totally mesmerised by Robin's words.

Robin's writing style is always from the heart, as a result it is so easy to feel exactly what she is feeling during her description of the scenarios and situations she is going through and experiencing. Robin is very honest and is always ready to be critical of own actions, if she needs to be. While reading the book I have felt that I am going through the journey with her and feel all her emotions and tribulations. I have often felt that Robin is sitting with me and interpreting and explaining to me the who, what, why this is all happening as though they are direct messages from the Divine just for me.

This book deals with one of the strongest emotions all us humans have and yet it can be so easily disguised as someone's nature or personality: that is the EGO. Such a small three lettered word, but this small word can destroy a person totally and not only this but everyone around them.

This book, right at the beginning, clearly explains how this ego is like a chameleon and it loves to be able to change itself and attach itself to all emotions, feelings and aspects of a person's life. The ego can cast a shadow on a person's life without the person's knowledge and giving them the false sense and understanding that this is part of their personality.

How often when we have done a good deed do we gloat or tell lots of people? Maybe you just gloat to yourself – see how wonderful I am. The good deed that you have just done, was this 'selfless,' as a deed should be, or was it 'selfish' just to make yourself feel good? As the saying goes 'just to massage your own ego'? It is so easy to get confused. I have started to think and reflect on my daily actions of what I do and ask myself was this selfless or selfish? Is it just to make me feel good about me or am I really helping the other person as work of the Divine. I have grown up in India with the belief which my Mum used to say, "Do a good deed then drop that thought into the water well, never to be spoken of again."

The opening scenario described so brilliantly in this book involve Robin helping her relative for an awfully long time. But this started to become a habit and the expectations started to rise from her relative. So, when it came time and her relative really needed help, patience was wearing thin, and the ego inside of Robin was fully kicking in. Robin describes all she felt at the time was anger and frustration, "I have done so much already, with no gratitude and often verbal abuse – I'm just so tired of all of this." We are all okay with giving surface or practical help because our ego allows us to feel so good about ourselves, but there is so much more to the ego's behavior as described in this book, it is mind blowing.

Reflecting on the surface help, but then realizing the consequences of her own actions (or lack of them) can sometimes cause us to expose our ego or put our "Ego on Front Street." Reflecting and evaluating her own actions, 'how could I have acted better….? Am I as good as I think I am – no I'm not.' Then going a step further, 'I thought I was a good Christian, what happened?' Then turning to the Divine (my favourite) and asking for guidance and realizing that the silent destroyer was still controlling her actions.

How beautifully Robin has described in this book the message from the Divine on exactly what it was she needed to do to support her relative in desperate need of help. Robin was divinely guided to wash her clothes, give her something to eat, a place to sleep, then take her to her church the next day and leave her there. This was so heart-wrenching for me to read and I felt quite tearful. This was only because at this point in the story neither Robin nor I could not understand the 'why' behind the guidance. We must remind ourselves, this must be for the best, because the Divine is never wrong. It was so difficult and painful for Robin. I could feel her pain jumping out of the pages of the book, but she did exactly, to the word, and followed the divine instructions. Such a brave woman! It is only afterwards; we realise why the Divine has instructed her to act in such a manner for the situation worked out better than anyone could have imagined.

The lesson learnt for me was to **TRUST in the Divine wholeheartedly without an ounce of doubt – always.**

Acknowledgements

You have often heard it said, "It takes a village to raise a child." Well, I would modify that statement to say, "It takes a village to anchor any new idea."

With that in mind, I would like to thank my friend and life coach Adele Green originally from South Africa, now living in Hawaii, for making this book a reality by being the first to believe in what I was doing and contributing money to help with publishing costs.

I would also like to thank my cousin Shelia Gammon of Philadelphia, PA for keeping me grounded through many crises and also contributing money to help make this book a reality.

All innovative ideas stay in the realm of unreality until you allow others to read and offer feedback as to the validity of the ideas. Many thanks to Shama Khurana who wrote the foreword and Kennesha Forrest who wrote the afterword for taking time to read a draft of this book. Your validation of many of the concepts in the book were much appreciated.

Special thanks to Danielle Bonnefil-Wahab, my tri-lingual editor and friend of 25 years for going that extra mile as my proofreader suggesting necessary corrections so the reader did not get sidetracked by focusing on the mistakes and miss the central message of the book.

There are those in life who continue to give you encouragement because they have traveled similar spiritual paths. To my life coaching friends Jeremy Lewis, Kristina Hess, Spring Lovell, Deborah Heist, India Johns and Madrid Jacobs-Brown, I thank you sincerely for sharing your stories and encouraging me to continue anchoring spiritual life coaching concepts in my own life.

Much is made of the role of family support; I am blessed to have incredibly supportive family members backing me up and testing out some of these concepts.

After the book is printed, it is useless unless people know about it, therefore I would like to thank my relatives Marcus Grasty and Nataly Torres for social media support.

I am grateful for the love and support of my mother, Shirley M. Dennis and my sisters, Pamela Johnson, and Sherrie Grasty.

Introduction

"Stop the madness" is a thought many people felt during the pandemic of 2020. The lifestyle so many had created was "unsustainable" which led many to want to make changes. Many found themselves tired…tired of the conflict…tired of the chaos…tired of the "have to" and the "should have." Even more became fed up with the thoughtless and aggressive way people treated them only to be quickly forgotten leaving many traumatized. That is why this book opens with chapters entitled, "I'm Sick of You," "Some Things Never Change," and "Enough is Enough." We have made so many allowances for people that we are no longer authentic within ourselves. At what point, do we stop asking the question "What's wrong with them" and look at the more fundamental question of "What's wrong with me for putting up with them?"

The slowdown of the pandemic gave people a chance to feel the unspoken emotional pain that being busy kept them from feeling. What is this "emotional pain" which often shows up as anger? To me it is "stuck negative emotional energy" of sadness, frustration, powerlessness, hopelessness, or even jealously. As a result of this emotional energy of victimization never being fully expressed, it often comes out in an explosion of anger. This helps temporarily with the internal pressure, but it does not give permanent voice to the many areas of emotional hurt. So residual negative emotional energy continues to build up again until the next explosion of anger. We must get to the root of the issues and release the emotional energy from that place. For doing that seems to disconnect the source of the negative energy from the behavior.

How do we access those parts of ourselves which will free us from the torment of our past? What role does our ego play? What do we need to change? How do we change? To what do we change to? An attempt will be made in this book to answer those questions. The change that most of us are seeking is a change from chaos and conflict to harmony and balance. There are conflicting ideas about how to achieve this. Some people believe that you need to identify your objectives, pursue them at all costs then you will be happy and fulfilled. Others believe you should take a step back, follow your intuitive guidance to your divine destiny. There is no right or wrong answer for how to move yourself forward. As I like to say, "Many roads lead to the summit."

In this book, I talk about just one of these roads. For myself, the road I decided to take was the spiritual path. To my surprise it required that I dig deeply into my human emotional self by digging deeply into my own ego. That was a surprise because I believed the "mind reigned supreme." All I needed to do was simply change my mind which would instantly bring me into spiritual alignment. This fundamental belief turned out to be "false" for me because no matter how hard I tried, "I could not make my mind take me where my heart did not want to go."

Sustaining my creations, I found was contingent upon me operating from my heart. Below the surface and superficial way of sharing kindness, there were overwhelming blockages in my heart from childhood trauma. It was through life coaching techniques, some of which I share in this book, that I was able to identify very distorted belief systems which came out of that trauma. It's hard to focus all your attention on trying to manifest a goal, when running underneath, in your subconscious mind, is a conflicting belief system telling you, "You're not valuable or worthy."

I don't know how one can simply wish away insecurity by focusing attention on some lofty desire.

At some point, if you are like me, then you can focus your attention long enough to accomplish your goal but once achieved, it is not possible to sustain or maintain what you have accomplished. It was to this that my mind went during the pandemic. What is it I need to do differently? What is hiding in my subconscious mind preventing me from maintaining my creations? Is my ego present in my procrastination? Am I delaying the writing this book, so I won't be disappointed but instead desire to live in the fantasy of its success? Why do I invite myself into someone else's world with ideas and suggestions then complain when I am asked to help execute them?

So many questions were flooding my mind, but the answers I sought were not found in the world. Believe me I tried to find them out there. I've traveled to over forty countries and studied most of the world's major religions. Yet, I was not able to live any of this spiritual philosophy which I believed would give my life synchronicity and flow. The answer was found on the "inner journey" I needed to take through the land of my hidden emotions. But that would mean I would have to get past the gatekeeper which was my "ego." How do I create a life that reflects who I truly am not who I created myself to be?

First, I had to admit that I was "not" being emotionally authentic to myself. The person I created myself to be was not the same person God created me to be. Once I admitted my deception, I could begin to take apart the facade of who I created myself to be. The facade was based upon my ego and my ego was based upon my childhood trauma.

Next, I had to uncover the patterns in my life. I am sure I am not the only one who has had a negative experience only to tell myself, "I will never let that happen again." What I learned in life coaching is this way of seeing reality is exactly what helps create our reality. Being on guard is what is magnetizing related incidents to us reinforcing our initial distorted belief. We then say, "see that is how people are." We must remember, our emotional energy is so strong that what we focus on expands even if the focus is on something negative. How many times after declaring, "I will never let that happen again," we experience similar episodes coming at us from all directions.

Finally, what if I told you, it was "not" necessary to be reactive to the same historic pain and fear? What if you could turn around to face whatever it was which was creating a problem for you? It is facing adversity that allows you to move your life in a new direction. Would it help to read about real live examples of making changes that have become permanent? Life does not have to be so hard.

This book was designed to be a useful guide offering processes you can replicate in your own lives. Whatever you are experiencing just know you are not alone. Many of us are trying to figure it out. I have found a way "out of the madness" that works for me. As you read my story, I think you will resonate with some of the situations I found myself in. Many are looking to make changes, but it requires each of us to give others more room to become who they need to be. It is this mindset that also frees us to become who we need to be. However, this process often requires you to expose your secrets by putting your "Ego on Front Street."

Chapter 1

I'm Sick of You

"I'm sick of you...You need to stop it" I yelled. "I can't take it anymore!" The response from my loved one was "You don't understand what it's like…I need help." My response again was "I don't care!" As I told you before "I can't continue to be target practice for your emotional outburst… you need to get it together." We went back and forth arguing with one another at 7:00 o'clock in the morning as the police arrived. Good, I am glad the police are here, now they can take control of the situation, I'm done.

The situation started at 5:30 a.m. when my loved one knocked on the door of one of the neighbors to request the neighbor's boyfriend move his car to the correct parking spot. The exchange got heated. As a result, I was sent a text message which I never saw, so I received a telephone call waking me up out of deep sleep. I am now agitated. Here I go again to deal with some situation that was not of my making.

"I'm so done," I thought to myself as I walked back across the parking lot to my apartment. I glanced back to see the police talking to my loved one. After entering my apartment, I pulled up a chair and watched the encounter from my window. At times, it was very animated on the part of my loved one. The police would ask a few questions and then nod. Suddenly, my loved one said something, threw up her hands then turned quickly walking away into her apartment. Whatever she said forced the police officers to rush in behind her. The next thing I saw was my loved one being led out of her apartment in handcuffs while still in her pajamas.

Be Careful What You Say

As my loved one was being ushered to the police car, I ran back outside to see what was going on. The police officer informed me that my loved one said, "she was going to commit suicide." I was not surprised because my loved one had been threatening that a lot lately. The only difference is that you must be careful what you say to police because they have a distinct set of rules by which they must abide. In my town, the threat of suicide requires the police to act ensuring the safety of the person.

The police instructed me to get my loved one's identification. As I returned with it, I locked her apartment door and stood transfixed for a few moments watching as if in a surreal movie as my loved one was put into the back of a police car in handcuffs. Then, like in slow motion, the police car rolled down the street turned disappearing out of sight. As I got back to my apartment, I thought to myself, "Oh my God, what just happened"? I felt a tinge of sadness, but mostly I felt waves of relief.

For the next couple of days, I thought it was like a joke whenever someone asked, "How is your loved one?" I would say, "I don't know." I am sure we will hear from her soon. Well, "Day 3" turned into "Day 4" with no word from her. I still don't know where she is or what's going on and nobody contacted her family.

Ego on Front Street

Now I'm starting to get concerned. Why wouldn't they call? Why wouldn't they tell the family something? Now more members of the family got involved as we started the search for her. It was at this point I had a moment of reckoning. I was no longer treating this situation as a joke. What if the last encounter I had with my loved one was the last time I was able to see her? That's when it hit me like a ton of bricks! For someone who thinks of themselves as so spiritual like I do, I realized some hard truths about myself in that moment. "I'm not that nice… I'm not that understanding… I'm not that supportive" then I burst into tears. Oh my God, my "Ego is on Front Street"!

That's the thought that came to me. "Ego on Front Street" to me comes when you drop the "mask of civility" you normally wear in favor of aggressive behavior in pursuit of your desires. Throughout this book, I'm using the term "Ego on Front Street" to mean that part of you when your behavior becomes so belligerent or aggressive in getting what you want that the situation can leave irreconcilable differences as relationships are fractured.

At this point in the story, my ego is on Front Street because I am supposed to be the spiritual one. Based on my Christian doctrine and my study at theology school, I am supposed to be the one who can "turn the other cheek" and "love your enemy." Despite my loved one saying several times that she "needed help," the only thing I thought about was "how I felt." Ego on Front Street!

Now that I don't know where my loved one is, and I don't know when I'll see her again, none of what I said during our last interaction still mattered. Now I am feeling the loss of her friendship. How often do we put ourselves in these situations where we say or do something out of anger? Our lack of concern for another person is magnified when some catastrophic event happens that does not allow us to take back what we said. Most of us believe we will always have another opportunity to alter a harsh remark we have projected onto another, but sometimes that is not always the case.

Even if nothing catastrophic happens, saying whatever is on your mind, not bothering to manage the anger coming out of your mouth because it is so deeply rooted within your heart can create what I call the "broken branch theory." When you break a branch, you can't put it back together. Sometimes harsh words spoken in anger and frustration can break the branch of a relationship. In some relationships it may mean they cannot be mended.

The Search is On

As we rolled into "Day 5" regarding my loved one, I finally found out what had happened. It started with shock and horror as we found out there was no record of her at the police station. We then heard there was no record of her at the local hospital's psychiatric ward.

When we couldn't find her any place, we reached out to a contact who worked in the mental health field who informed us that in these situations, people threatening suicide can be taken to the state hospital for a psychiatric evaluation.

As a last resort, a call was made to the state hospital. When they answered, they would neither "confirm nor deny" her presence there. Fortunately, the family heard from her shortly after that call. As for me, I finally felt relief knowing what had happened to her. I was grateful that my previous encounter with her was not going to be my last.

Chapter 2

Some Things Never Change

Unfortunately, when my loved one got out of the state hospital not much had changed regarding her behavior. She came back just as belligerent and aggressive as when she left. This is when the landlord said, "enough is enough." I feel much compassion for people who deal with mental health in their families. Unless you have the experience first-hand, you never know how you will react. It is irritating and frustrating along with virtually impossible to "make" someone behave in "appropriate ways." What you need them to do will go undone unless that is what they wish or desire for themselves.

In some ways, those with mental health issues display an "ego on steroids." Without warning during normal conversations, there can be an "emotional explosion" like a volcano where resentment and unspoken emotionality which had been compartmentalized comes rushing to the surface for release. That is what happened to me during the last encounter I had with my loved one before she went to the state hospital. I was so full of rage and frustration at her for being victimized by her anger that I could no longer contain it. That is why I was engaged in a shouting match when the police arrived.

Storage Bin is Full

It's important to know we all carry residual emotionality which comes from the fact that life happens at such a fast paced we are not always able to process our own emotions. For the unprocessed, unexpressed, and unhealed emotion it tends to be stored away or compartmentalized in such a way it no longer interferes with our daily functioning. However, it is still there nonetheless in the background waiting to be dealt with. As life continues to show us trauma and drama then more of this unhealed, unspoken, and unexpressed emotionality can get stored.

At some point in all of us the storage bin gets full, and it must be emptied. Most of us do not know when the "storage bin is full" so we do not know how much more we can take. Therefore, it is often the "straw that breaks the camel's back" when something little happens that does not require the kind of emotional reaction we show. An opening of anger and frustration allows for some of the unhealed emotion to also come up creating an intensity that is way more than the current situation calls for. Unfortunately, the intensity causes the other person to be triggered and defensive unloading emotional energy as well from their storage bin which is also full.

How do we get ourselves to that place where we can be emotionally authentic able to respond in real time to situations in which we are feeling angry? It is not just about anger. Remember, anger can cover a multitude of negative feelings such as sadness, powerlessness, or despair. How do we express ourselves in such a way that it does not result in the kind of confrontation and chaos that is too often witnessed in the world? It is to this concept that I have turned my attention. I have tried to come at this problem by blending spirituality and life coaching.

Pressing Pause on Spiritual Philosophy

From a spiritual perspective, many of us on the spiritual journey are trying hard to control our emotional body. We do not want our emotions to overtake us because we are often busy trying to adhere to spiritual principles. Some of this spiritual philosophy such as "love your enemies" or "turn the other cheek" create obstacles for us when we have real emotional reactions to the wrong that someone is doing to us. How do you reconcile "turning the other cheek" when every fiber of your being is telling you to "knock somebody out"? How do you reconcile "love your enemy" when you have given someone the benefit of the doubt repeatedly only to be used and abused?

As humans, we have a way of seeing reality that will "not" allow us to freely express our emotions while practicing our spiritual beliefs. One of the reasons I got into life coaching was because there did not appear to be enough room in the study of spirituality which allowed for the interplay with the "emotional body." I was often stuck in striving to live my spiritual philosophy because I could not accept "what I feel doesn't matter." How do I reconcile being "Ok" with being abused? Some of these questions are profound.

As we continue this journey together, we're going to talk more about this because this is an area that many on the spiritual path get "tripped up." Denying our emotions will only get us so far before anger and frustration set in from suppressing authentic emotionality. Therefore, I say sometimes, you might have to press pause on your spiritual philosophy to allow your authentic feelings to surface. This is what happened with me and my loved one on the day the police arrived.

Let's Step Back in Time

The anger and frustration for me towards my loved one was building through a series of incidents over several years. Even though I was often told by my loved one that her behavior was not "intentional," it did not help when I felt attacked. It is like being cut and bleeding then having someone tell you not to pay attention to the pain is like being victimized all over again. Verbal attacks can cut through your emotional body just like a knife can cut through your physical body with both leaving scares which need healing. Telling someone your behavior was not intentional may mitigate their immediate response, but it does not eliminate their pain. The only thing that can help is for the perpetrator to express remorse or apology then focus on what motivated their own behavior while giving the other person time and space to heal.

Now, let's get back to the current story. Earlier that summer, I received a call from my loved one who asked me if I could take her to get her medications. I agreed. As we were riding to the pharmacy, she informed me that she didn't have enough money to get her medication. At that moment, I felt a wave of anger rising inside of me. I was sick of feeling responsible for her. I responded in a curt voice as I said, "What do you mean you don't have enough money for your medication"! I went on to ask, "How can you not have enough money to take care of something so important when you just received your disability check"?

Well, I knew the answer to the question which is what also fueled my anger. One of the reasons she did not have enough money is because she was running a tab at the local liquor store that she settled without failure every month. This left her with little or no money to do basic things like purchase her own medication. That in and of itself should have told me the level of danger she was already in, but I was in my feelings and just mad because it was an inconvenience for me. I was not looking at what was going on with her because here again the ego only looks out for itself.

As we arrived at the store, I contributed to the payment of her medication but I'm fuming mad, so I don't say much. As a matter fact, on the ride back, I didn't say anything for about three blocks, and we only had to travel four blocks. Finally, I spoke in a solemn voice and said, "The way you are living is unsustainable… you need to get some help… you need to make some changes in your life." At that point, after being quiet for a few minutes, she responded by saying "you're right, I agree." That's how we left that conversation.

Treatment Failure

A few days later she asked me if I would go with her as she checked herself into the local hospital for a psychiatric evaluation. She was aware of her diagnosis of bipolar disorder and knew that her current medication regime needed updating. One of the issues pushing her behavior was that her main medication she had been taking for 30 years was no longer being offered because it was addictive. Unknowingly to the rest of us, my loved one went without the medication rather than follow the doctors request to switch to a new medication which would have required hospitalization to wean her off the old medication because of the potential withdraw symptoms.

Understanding all of this, I went with her as she checked herself into the hospital. Everything went well for a few weeks. She was soon released to another facility as a transition to ensure new medication was working well. Since she was not only my loved one but also my neighbor, she made agreements with me and the landlord to do certain things upon her return to the property which would lesson disruptions to the other tenants. We were hopeful we had put this chapter behind us.

It is with great anticipation I went to pick her up. I loaded the car with all her stuff, but she kept me waiting while she smoked a cigarette. I could feel my anger rising but tried to keep it "in check." She got in the car but within two blocks of leaving the facility, she was speaking to me in that old aggressive and belligerent tone as she started telling me off! Oh no, not another treatment failure. The anger that came over me was more like rage. I don't know where it came from but the only words that I could get out of my mouth were "Shut Up. I am not doing this." There must have been something in my tone because she shut up immediately as we drove to the apartment complex in silence.

Here We Go Again

As the silence continued, I helped her unpack her stuff then parked the car. I was so glad to be able to go into my own apartment as she went into hers. As far as I was concerned that was the end of our interaction. But it wasn't the end because a few minutes later I heard her enter the side door. She went down the hallway and into the kitchen door to visit with the landlord. It was quiet for a moment then suddenly I could hear my loved one hollering and screaming at the 80-year landlord! I couldn't hear the details of what was said, I just know the tone in which it was said. Here we go again. Unfortunately, I did not have the energy to go and interfere. The good news was my loved one did not stay long.

What's interesting about encounters with my loved one is that once she was finished blowing off this angry energy, she was the nicest person you would ever want to meet. She was funny, joyful, kind, generous and overall awesome. However, the darkness she carried was unbelievable. When triggered, she didn't even look like the same person. As the darkness descended over her, the whites of her eyes would disappear giving way to only black coals staring back. Even her face contorted to comply with the rage. Be careful if you were in her sights when she was triggered because she would use your vulnerabilities to verbally attack you. It was absolutely amazing to witness how quickly she could move between darkness and light.

Chapter 3

Enough is Enough

Every few days there seemed to be something else until that fateful morning at 7:00 AM when the police arrived. That event was going to be the third stop to a mental health facility in 60 days. No matter what accommodations we made, we could "not" make a difference for her. That helpless, powerless feeling is really a sad state to be in but the mental health of everyone in the apartment complex was being challenged by the ongoing verbal attacks. That is when the landlord made the hard decision that it was time for my loved one to find new accommodations.

In the meantime, it was decided I would drive her to a temporary shelter that my loved one had found through a non-profit housing agency. Within a few days of having dropped my loved one off, I went out of town to a funeral of my great-aunt. It was bittersweet as many of the cousins sat around talking about shared memories. It was a very emotional time between the funeral and activities back home all of which left me drained.

I was lulled into a false sense of security since I had not heard from my loved one in a few days, I assumed all was well at the emergency shelter. Even though the shelter had room for her, she was not finished being triggered and dictating terms through her anger. She was still in rare form as she unloaded on people in this new environment. Her ego was stronger than ever. But before the week was out, the shelter with it rules that she was consistently violating "put her out"! Now she was officially "homeless" and made her way back to the apartment complex and set up a temporary shelter in the stairwell.

God's Ways Are Not Our Ways

All the way back home on the flight, given that I am a spiritual person, I was asking God "What should I do with my loved one"? This is the first time I had ever really asked the question without coming from a place of reaction. The information that came back to me was astounding. You see I am clairaudient which means I can hear the "still small voice" of my Spirit as easily as listening to another person. What I was not prepared for was the message.

I was told by my Spirit that when I see her that I should wash her clothes, clean her up, take her to get something to eat, give her a place to sleep, give her some money, and the next morning take her with all her belongings to her church. I repeated that information back to my Spirit several times because in my human mind this seemed cold and unfeeling. To me it felt like I was putting my loved one back out into homelessness. How is that a good thing? At this point, a thought popped into my head which was part of a quote from the Holy Bible which says, "God's ways are not our ways." So, with that in mind, knowing I had no answers, I decided to trust the divine guidance I was being given.

When I came home, I opened the door to the stairwell and stared at the sight of homelessness. It was sad to see how disheveled she was as she started talking rapidly. I knew what I needed to do so I told her give me a few minutes and I would get back to her. I took a minute to center myself and asked for spiritual guidance as I implemented what I was being guided to do. I stayed calm as I asked her for one thing at a time starting with her laundry. Everything got done and I told her of the plan for the next day to take her to church. We stayed up most of the night talking and I told her everything would be "OK" if she just followed the divine guidance she was getting from God. She said she understood. One of the last things she said is that her unruly behavior, which left her homeless, now required her to put her "Ego on Front Street." If she didn't reign it in, she would forever be homeless.

An Ending Unlike No Other

I guess you would like to know how the story ends. I will just say that "nothing is as it appears to be." As we packed her bags for church, I told her that the forecast predicts it was going to rain that day. So, after church if she didn't have anywhere else to go that she should walk to the local train station which would provide cover for her. It was a small structure with a bench, windows, but no door. At least in her "homeless state," she would not be on the street getting wet. Also from this location, she could change her clothes at the local McDonald's just two blocks away. When we arrived at the church, I reminded her to store her belongings first then take a seat and participate in the church service. After that she could figure out what she most needed.

As I drove off, I felt a sense of calm as I remembered thinking, "God this is in your hands now as I've done what you told me to do… I have no idea how this is going to work out but if this is what you told me to do it should be OK." It is easy to have spiritual philosophy, but can you truly apply it when everything within you wants to do something differently than you are being divinely guided to do. Not only was this time challenging for my loved one, but it was also the ultimate test of my faith.

I did not hear from my loved one that day but heard from her the next day. When I heard her voice, she sounded happy. I asked what happened? She began to explain that after the church service concluded, she went downstairs where they served refreshments. She told her pastor she needed help and the biggest help he could give her was to purchase her a cell phone. The pastor agreed. While he went to the store to get her a burner cell phone, she had the nicest conversation with a couple while she waited for the pastor to come back.

When he returned with the phone, the nice couple asked her where they could drop her. She replied that she was going to the local train station. So, they loaded her bags in their car and took her to the train station. Before letting her out, they asked where she was going? They were stunned and surprised when said "nowhere, I'm homeless." Even though she did not know them, they told her, "We are not leaving you here." They took her home with them. She stayed with them for the next 30 days until she was able to locate new permanent housing. Even though her new housing would be in a different town, the facility would provide food, shelter, laundry services, and medication management. My loved one could afford all if it on her income.

It Pays to Listen

The biggest lesson I got out of this experience is that there really is a God whose ways are not our ways. We don't always need to figure out what's going, sometimes all we need to do is just listen. All of us have a part to play in the lives of others but it is important to remember there are bigger forces at work. My loved one and I would both agree that putting your "Ego on Front Street" may require you to be put in situations which you cannot get back from. When that happens, it forces you to make some decisions about whether you're willing to change or continue to follow your aggressive, belligerent, confrontational ego which keeps reinforcing separation and isolation.

At some point, we all get confronted with this choice, but we don't know what our options are. How do you follow your spirit? What does that look like? As you give up your personal agenda as championed by ego to follow divine guidance then all other decisions flow easily from that choice. After a few years away, my loved one has now returned to reside in the complex once again. She is a model citizen and an asset to everyone. She will be the first to tell you that the path she took to get her "ridiculous behavior" under control required her to put her "Ego on Front Street."

Chapter 4

Self-Sacrifice Not Required

You've just read the story so you understand how devastating a person's ego can be. Let's talk about how the ego is created and the role it plays. For purposes of this book, references to the ego are arrogant and narcissistic behaviors that can consume individuals with beliefs like, "this works for me, so it should be fine for you" or "I know what is best." To me, the ego is that part of us that is birthed out of the emotional pain and trauma of childhood where beliefs are created.

It is the part of us that plays the role as our "protector" when we are experiencing powerless situations. Our ego becomes our guide in surviving a world full of uncertainty, chaos, and conflict as it tries to restore control and safety. It's ironic that the persona of the ego can be arrogance because the shadow side of arrogance is "insecurity." The job of the ego is to navigate in such a way as to make sure what happened to us, never happens again but it never accounts for our growth and development.

There is little tolerance for anyone mistreating our ego or not seeing and complying with its needs. The ego uses many different approaches in the role it plays. For some like my loved one, her ego used belligerence and aggression to force compliance. Whereas for me and many on a spiritual path, our egos are a lot more manipulative. We tend to use our altruism, niceness, and kindness as a tool to get people to do for us what we want, even if that is to be praised for helping. As I said before, the ego is all about itself, not other people.

Self-Sacrifice Anchors Ego

For those on a spiritual path, you need to ask the question even when you think you are doing something good, "What's the payoff for me"? Too often being good means "sacrificing yourself to do good." In this new way of being, self-sacrifice is "not" required because it is a recipe for disaster. There is no way to sacrifice yourself, repeatedly for the best interest of others, without this "way of being" eventually causing you resentment towards those you help. Serving to the point of being out of balance fuels the ego until it is ready to explode.

In addition, don't be too quick to compromise on what you genuinely want for this too fuels the ego. Let me give you an example. I was in the grocery store with a relative. She went down the isle of household cleaning supplies looking for air freshener. She found what she wanted, but the refills only came in a twin pack when she needed three refills. She instantly went for the cheaper triplet pack to save $2 all the while saying how she did "not" like that fragrance. I urged her to get the twin pack and we found a single of the same fragrance.

I told her if she compromised, then she would be agitated and irritated which she would then project onto me. I continued by saying, "If I call you about something, you will have an attitude with me, causing an unnecessary confrontation. All of this would happen because you compromised on air freshener which would be fueling your displeasure." She responded, "You are right," as we both burst into a hearty laughter.

The ego has created a thought system which has us believing the opposite of what is true. It has us believing lack is sufficient because we must share. It has us believing safety and security rest in attack. Then, the ego's thought system can be hypocritical as it has us believing "only what I want matters" all the while promoting we can live in harmony with others. If I get what I want and you don't, what kind of harmony will that produce? Or if I sacrifice myself for you, and you don't sacrifice for me, will that make me happy. How?

Filtering Reality

The way our ego functions and the thought system it has created is insane, but we don't even see it like that. It is rooted in such a way, grounded in such a way that it uses our conditioning, so we don't even know it's there. We don't know we have these beliefs that control our behavior. Based upon our perception, all we know is "it shouldn't be like that." We judge everything we see because that's our conditioning.

Let's talk psychology for a moment where it is agreed that everything we see comes out of our conditioning (values, religion, education, race, culture, country, and experiences). So, the way we were raised or the neighborhood we grew up in are some of the variables that come together to create a filter through which we see reality. Now add to this filter your individual experiences of trauma which bring additional limiting beliefs. Based upon our conditioning with this added filter, no wonder many of us are so "messed up."

Messed Up

I will speak for myself. "I'm really messed up and I'm clear I'm messed up." Based upon conditioning and filtering of reality, can you admit you are messed up too? Using the formula I gave you for conditioning, let me show you how I was affected by early trauma. Ready…Here goes…

I was born in the U.S. as an African American in Philadelphia in the late 1950's. I was fortunate enough to have been born into a family with two parents and an older and younger sister. We lived in a close-knit neighborhood of upwardly mobile African Americans. Grounded in church on Sundays and civil rights meetings during the week, I was programed for the world I was to grow up in.

Since my father divorced my mother when I was 3 years old, I grew up with a lot of responsibility from an early age. Needless to say, I did not always meet my obligations. That resulted in what they called "spankings" from guardians. The problem with some of the spankings was that I was punished not only for the things I did wrong, but also for the things my siblings did wrong. I call this the "peer accountability model." The problem with this model is it left me with a feeling of an "exaggerated sense of responsibility for the behavior of others" to avoid punishment for myself.

Now overlay my sexual assault trauma with my conditioning then I am left with a toxic stew of emotions raging inside of me before age 8. I had become unable to express my authentic emotionality around the situations that were happening to me. I felt powerless, hopeless, helpless, and victimized. Having to operate day in and day out allowed this residual emotion to be build inside of me without having a way out.

Adults around me were overloaded with their own responsibilities and were not always interested in how "I was feeling." When I did express my anger or frustration, it was sometimes met with "I don't care… handle it." It was not their intention, but unfortunately for me the conditioning taught me that "I don't matter" yet "I am responsible for the behavior of others." What do you think happened to me when I took this fundamental way of seeing reality out into the adult world? Well, that is a book for another time!

Early Conditioning Matters

What most of us don't understand is that who we are is because of what has happened to us. We see things a certain way and we do things the way we do things because of early conditioning. It is unfortunate that given all that has happened to us, there is not a process to unscramble the distorted beliefs before we go out into the world as young adults. I'm not three… I'm not five… I'm not ten… but I still function with a childlike perspective on the world. I know this way of being is no longer working for me anymore yet, I was never taught how to dissolve the ego's attachment which is controlling the filters through which I see reality.

The science has said that before age 7, the brain of a child only operates in a "theta state". During this time, children are connected to their internal world of imagination and daydreaming without the ability to use critical or rational thinking. So, everything that happens to us is just recording and socializing us to live in the world of the future. Unfortunately, this conditioning will be running in our subconscious minds as the default program when we become adults. This is what makes changing the way we function so difficult after we become grown.

With subconscious programming being so powerful, I'm surprised I am a high functioning adult given some of the traumatic experiences I have had growing up. In so many ways, my life was normal because it wasn't traumatic every day. But there was enough trauma to create glitches in the programming.

I See Only the Past

How do we do this? How do we unscramble ourselves and detach from our ego? How do we correct the distorted beliefs created from those early experiences? For an answer, I turn to one of my favorite books called "A Course in Miracles." In the workbook section, it refers to some concepts which I think can help us here. The initial lessons cover themes such as: nothing that I see means anything... I have given everything all the meaning that it has... I am not upset for the reason that I think... I am upset because I see something that's not there... I see only the past. Wow, that is something to think about. What if we really owned the idea that everything we see, is based up our past conditioning and we see nothing as it is right now?

Therein lies the problem for humanity. Most of us are operating through the "filters of our past." We see nothing as it is right now but instead, we are "shadow boxing" or "sleepwalking" through life. The ways we are reacting to the behavior others comes from our past conditioning. Therefore, through our ego which functions to protect us, we're going to get in front of any potential hurt, harm, or danger. The ego's plan is to stop anybody who acts like they are about to do the same thing that caused us pain in the past. We tend not see anything as it is now.

We don't see the strength that we have developed over time. We don't see we are not the same people who were powerless in the face of previous incidents. The dominant way most of us function is through the heavy dark filters of our past. We need to begin to acknowledge "nothing that we see means anything" and "we are giving everything all the meaning that it has."

Judge Not

To create space to change our thought system, we must pull back on our need to judge and criticize everything and everybody including ourselves. So how do we stop judging? Well let's come at it from a different angle, "Why do we judge"? I can't speak for everybody but as for why I judge it is because it keeps me in the driver seat of control which is necessary if I am not to be punished. I judge what others are doing to ensure they cover all the potential outcomes which could be detrimental to me. Since I have been programmed to take the blame for things going wrong, whether it was my decision or not, I am overbearing and extremely critical of others. It is also easy to point the finger at others so that I am not the one under the microscope.

What happens when we judge someone as "less than"? Being able to criticize or judge others provides a big payoff for our ego giving it energy. Judgement and criticism are vital for our ego's survival because it needs to be fed with feelings of superiority from setting the standards for others to meet. So, the ego gets fed through confrontation because others are not meeting our standards. The tension then causes division. The whole point of the ego structure is for it to keep us in silos which are separate and apart from one another. The ego does not benefit from everybody getting along because the ego sees everybody else's needs as in competition with its own.

Chapter 5

Speed Requires Alignment

The emotional body is particularly important in helping us to navigate our reality. It is the emotional body that gives us the additional information we need to make decisions. What happens if the emotional body is limited in its ability to function due to past conditioning or trauma? What happens if the heart has become closed down and unable to feel?

Let's use the analogy of a car in terms of how it operates to further explain how limitations can negatively impact functioning. There is nothing more exhilarating than getting into a car on a bright sunny day, experiencing endless joy speeding down an open highway. Nothing beats the warm breezes that come with the windows down. It is easy to ride in a vehicle that has full alignment. There is no worry if you only have one hand on the steering wheel that the car will run off the road. In so many ways, our emotional body is like that of a car as it too needs to be aligned. The alignment for the emotional body is often positive emotions like happiness, joy, and love which move us easily towards our destiny.

Misalignment from Potholes

There is more likelihood of damage when a car is no longer traveling down an open highway but traveling in the inner city? Attention must now be paid to a lot more traffic as well as being mindful of more potholes. What happens to your car after repeatedly hitting potholes? Some may say, there is the potential for a flat tire. Others may say, you run the risk of breaking your axel. However, the biggest nuisance problem most drivers face after hitting potholes is that the car is no longer in alignment. All drivers know the feel of their car when they are no longer in alignment because the car will pull towards one side. You can feel it in the steering wheel.

It takes a lot more energy to control your car when it's out of alignment. First, you tend to put two hands on the steering wheel with more pressure on one side of the steering wheel to balance it from drifting. Next, once you've hit several potholes, you are now more conscious of other potholes upcoming. You find yourself watching the road as you travel looking for patches that look uneven alerting you to potential potholes. The goal now is to avoid them, so you also tend to drive more cautiously because you don't want to hit another pothole. You may not go as fast as you would normally go and gone are the days of feeling carefree in your car.

Well, if we take this analogy and extend it to our emotional body then some of the same principles hold. To be able to ride down the road carefree in our emotional body means that we are fueled up and in alignment. But if we have hit too many potholes in life, meaning we have too many traumas, then our emotional alignment will be off. Some of our unresolved issues then affect our alignment so we no longer trust our own emotions to help navigate us. Unconsciously, we may end up pulling the emotional body towards one side tending towards overly cautious.

Controlling Out of Fear

As many of you know, "fear is an anticipatory emotion" not a current reality. We are not afraid of what we "know," we are afraid of what we "don't know." From this place, if we perceive a situation as negative, hurtful, or harmful then our emotional body can no longer navigate effectively. It is more difficult to get from where we are to where we want to go. We become awfully slow and cautious about our interactions with everything and everybody due to some of the potholes we have hit along the way that brought us out of emotional alignment.

Whether you are moving in the world in a car or in your emotional body, the biggest issue with trying to control a vessel that is out of alignment is the energy and effort it takes. If we are putting our energy and effort into trying to control, we cannot freely enjoy what is happening. We are not present because our attention is elsewhere. If you think about it, the pothole we hit or the trauma we experienced that has led to the alignment issues is really in the past. It is only affecting our current reality because we have not dealt with it.

We need to release this stuck emotionality, because as it was said before, this is where the "ego goes to hide." There are a few clues that can tell you if you are out of emotional alignment drifting into another lane or about to crash into someone. If you are having a confrontation with someone but you cannot see that you are the one initiating the contact, then you have a problem. From your perspective, you think the crash is being precipitated by someone else. The truth is because of your emotional alignment issues, it is allowing your vehicle to drift into another lane. You are the one causing the accident or confrontation.

In life coaching we often say, "the only person you cannot see is yourself." So, the best way to see yourself is through the eyes of other people. For instance, if you see yourself as loving, kind, generous and understanding but nobody else sees those characteristics in you then you have much work to do. But if how you see yourself is mirrored back to you from the world, then it confirms your emotional alignment.

It is important to talk to some people who know you to see if any of those characteristics you value are being seen by others. If they don't see them then you can believe somewhere your emotional alignment is off. Without alignment there is no possibility of momentum. As I said before when a car is out of alignment you must go slow, continually checking in your rearview mirror to be sure you get out of the way of somebody who is moving faster.

Sunglasses Distort Reality

To be slow and cautious is what we do when we have emotional trauma that is unhealed. Slow and cautious it how we function with an eye on the past. From an emotional place we are living in the past and projecting it into the current moment. So, what does that mean if you have trauma that is "unhealed"? You are hyper-sensitive to certain situations so as not to re-experience similar trauma. That is a normal human reaction.

In spiritual circles we say that "where attention goes, energy flows." So ironically, in trying to be so conscious of past trauma not reoccurring, your attention often magnetizes related traumas. In so many ways by magnetizing similar events it reinforces the initial distorted belief. It is like putting on a pair of sunglasses which create a filter then depending on how heavy that filter is we complain about the contrasting colors. Reds aren't as red as they need to be, and blues don't stand out the way they should because colors are not as vibrant as we think they should be.

We don't understand through living our life under the guidance of our ego that we have now selected a pair of sunglasses. Some of us have chosen filters so dark that some colors cannot be seen at all. That is, we may block out the "good" that life can show us because we are always thinking about how "someone is going to use us" or "demand payment." We are feeding our energy into the thing we most fear then magnetizing it to ourselves. We have more power over our thoughts than we are giving ourselves credit for. If you don't like the reality you are seeing, you can choose a different filter by healing your emotional body.

We now know the ego hides behind the sunglasses of criticism and judgement which are the filters your ego uses to keep you out of emotional alignment. How do we bring ourselves back into alignment? That's a good question. What do you do with a car when you want to bring it into alignment? You take it to a Body Shop where there are experts who can look at that the alignment issues to determine where the problem is. The mechanic knows what to look for to adjust the car. Once you get your car back, you can now accelerate with no hands if you want, and the car will go in the direction in which you point it. The car doesn't drift or pull any longer because the alignment has been corrected.

There is nothing better than driving a car that is in alignment and the same can be said for our emotional bodies. They must be put back into alignment using various methods. Just like with a car, outside help can be obtained to gain a new perspective. Remember, the ego is a chameleon which can rapidly morph and change until it is unrecognizable. Another person may be able to help identify your unhealed trauma before some catastrophe happens to expose your ego.

Chapter 6

Bumps and Potholes

Sometimes it takes a minute to find out what has happened to you to force your misalignment. Sometimes you may not know, or you cannot see what the events were that forced the misalignment. All of us move through life having traumas occur and we deal with them as best we can. To the world it appears we have moved on but internally each of these bumps in the road is a pothole.

If we continue with our car analogy, if we are hitting the same wheel as we drive down the road then at some point the alignment will be affected. When the car goes in for alignment, we don't necessarily know which wheel is really the problem, only the mechanic can help diagnose that accurately. Similarly, the belief that has come out of the trauma needs to be diagnosed, it's not necessarily the trauma in and of itself that is problematic, but the resulting distorted beliefs are. Traumas produce those moments when you say to yourself, "I'm never going to let this happen again."

The beliefs coming out of the trauma such as: I'm never going to let someone mistreat me; I'm never going to let someone disrespect me; I'm never going to let someone say that to me; or I'm never going to let someone do that to me. All these kinds of beliefs are causing emotional misalignment and are unfairly being projected onto others who had nothing to do with creating that belief in the first place.

Can't Catch a Break

Let me give you an example of projecting distorted beliefs. Right out of college I was dating "Mr. Tall, Dark, and Handsome." He was absolutely fueling my emotional body through love, fun, and adventure. The beginning of a relationship is simply wonderful as you can barely sleep because you are so excited by the presence of another person.

Well as time went on, we hit a few speed bumps and a few potholes. It was not as easy and as comfortable in our relationship. What started to happen was there were times when I would ask my friend, "Are you coming back tonight?" He would often answer "Yes." I'd ask what time so I could take care of other things while he was gone. He would give a time but repeatedly and routinely would "not" show back up. This often led to arguments but given the charmer that he was, he was always able to smooth things over. He would promise to change his behavior and for a while he would act appropriately. Eventually, he would go back to the original pattern of being late or not showing up at all. The real problem I finally found out was that he had another girlfriend.

The emotional reaction to this pattern of promising and not following through created an emotional alignment issue for me which eventually led to our breakup. Now here is the rub. This is when undigested emotional pain can be projected. Unfortunately, the next guy that I dated caught some attitudes not really meant for him.

For the new guy, we set the time for 6:00 p.m. right after work to meet for dinner. Because I lived and worked near downtown Atlanta, it took me no time to get home. I had plenty of time to relax and was excited about the date. As the 6 p.m. hour approached, I began to be on the lookout for him. By 6:10 there was still no sign of him, and I assumed he got caught in traffic. So why didn't I text him or call him? Well, this date was happening way before cellphones. I kept my eye on the time which moved slowly from 6:15 to 6:30.

That is when I heard a knock on my door. I cannot tell you the state that I was in by then. I was angry and unwilling to hear him out as he kept trying to explain his tardiness. He didn't understand why I was so upset about him being late since it was not intentional. He was clueless about the intensity I was directing at him. Poor guy could not catch a break. Simply put, I was projecting my anger onto him that was really meant for somebody else. The anger that got triggered in me was really for my last boyfriend who was always late. Because I exploded on my new friend, I can tell you I did "not" get a second date.

Time to Fix Our Emotional Alignment

I share this example to show how easily our emotions are exploding creating a level of intensity that has little to do with other people. The situation we find ourselves in is triggering an old wound within us. It is time we fix our emotional alignment. All issues that are unresolved and all secrets that have never been reconciled are the fuel that the ego uses to keep us driving off the road in our relationships.

It is time for us to get the help we individually and collectively need so we can begin to use our GPS in a helpful way. In the new cars they have not only GPS, but they also have "park assist." With GPS, all you need to do is program where you desire to go, and your car will take you there. Now they even have cars that let you get where you are going while driving hands free if you're willing to be so bold. In addition to GPS, the upgrades in technology for cars allows you to have park assist. This means if you are not very good at squeezing into tight parking places or good at parallel parking on the street, you can just ask the car to help you park as you let go of the wheel.

The same way a car has GPS, we too as humans have a divine guidance system which we need to put ourselves back in touch with. The way to access this system is to clear the emotional body of unresolved issues and distorted beliefs. Sometimes, it might require us to confront the people who took our power to release us from the fear. In spiritual circles, we would often say that "fear" is an acronym meaning "False Evidence Appearing Real." The ego thrives on fear because the "ego" as we also say in spiritual circles stands for "Easing God Out."

As we clear our emotional channels, letting go of our secrets, we can once again have God as our GPS. If God is navigating, we will always know where we are going. We will also know how we will get there and by when. Once we arrive, we will always have "park assist" to help us get into or out of tight spaces. We will know how to navigate anything and everything in our current reality without the need to look backwards. No frame of reference will be needed if God is your GPS.

Various methods can be used to bring your emotional body back into alignment. The most important thing is to find someone with whom you can share your secrets. For it is the unhealed secrets which fuel anger and therefore fuel the ego. Traditional methods such as seeing a therapist can be extremely useful depending on the level of the trauma. You can engage in "talk therapy" with a life coach, family, or friends. If you lean towards the spiritual, you can get pastoral counseling. Some people find relief in "EFT" tapping techniques. As for me, I am an enthusiastic fan of "inner child" work where you track the root causes of your behavior back to your wounded "inner child." My other favorite technique is getting up the courage to emotionally confront the person who took my power. Any combination of the suggestions above can help you finally "let go" of what is holding you.

Chapter 7

Enjoying Amusement Parks

Life is funny. Sometimes under ego guidance, it feels like we are living life in an amusement park. What is nice is that amusement parks have different themes. For instance, at Disney World there are four major theme parks such as: Magic Kingdom, Epcot, Hollywood Studios, and Animal Kingdom. Within each park are a variety of different rides providing thrilling experiences.

In so many ways our lives are just like that, full of ups/downs and twists/turns through unanticipated adventures. The way we experience our reality comes from the lenses we wear. If we are looking through spiritual lenses, we experience rides that are fun, harmonious, peaceful, and joyful. But, if we are looking through the distorted lenses of our ego, the rides we take are often scary, heart-stopping, stressful and anxiety filled.

Everybody's life has a theme. What's the theme of your life? What is it that you are forever trying to experience? Are you trying to get somebody to help you? Are you trying to get somebody to acknowledge you? Are you trying to get somebody to support you? Everybody has a theme because very few of us see ourselves as whole and complete just as we are. Therefore, everybody is striving to get somebody to complete them. For the lucky few, they are taking rides in a different theme park because they understand the "essential essence" of who God made them to be. They feel whole and complete taking immense joy in sharing from their abundance of love and prosperity.

If You Love Me

The untold truth is that all of us are already whole and complete. But we see ourselves as "incomplete" with an eye on what is missing or lacking from our lives. Therefore, we spend our time on stressful rides needing someone to do "X" so we can experience "Y." If we don't get what we want, then we try to guilt, bully, or manipulate someone into compliance. In our twisted minds, how could someone refuse us.

The conversation of requests goes something like this: "If you love me, then you will want to make me happy" … "If you love me, you will want to please me" … "If you love me, you will make what I want a priority." But if everyone is making this demand, who is left to fulfill the orders? This way of thinking is insane as we think it logical that someone fulfill our desires even if it means hurting themselves. We often ask people to sacrifice themselves for us, but rarely are we willing to do the same for them.

Our amusement park rides are anxiety-ridden because we are waiting on external validation of our "lovability." We place way too much attention on what it means about your love for me if you refuse me. "If you have something else to do that's more important, then it means you don't love me." We have put ourselves in a box because we are following ego guidance with respect to our worthiness with these false statements of causality.

When you take back control of your life and live from a place of wholeness, one of the things you consider is putting your "Ego on Front Street." This begins to disentangle you from the whiplash that comes from trying to please others as a way of surviving. When you are willing to expose your ego, you have reached a place of truth and authenticity. When I reached this place in an intense argument with my loved one, I had to finally admit some truths: I'm not that good…I'm not that kind…I'm not that generous…I'm not that supportive…I'm not that loving.

Being able to admit to the negative aspects of yourself publicly and openly allow you to loosen the grip of your ego. When you can "unapologetically" say to another person "count me out" when responding to ego demands, then your options at the amusement park have just expanded exponentially.

I Can Do That

Just because you put your "Ego on Front Street" regarding some aspect of your life, don't believe that is the end of it. Remember, the ego is a chameleon and can shift and morph in ways that are amazing and astounding. I want to give a heads-up to my spiritual friends, ego loves fooling you. If you want to be spiritual, the ego says, "I can do that." If you want to appear altruistic and loving, the ego says, "I can do that." If you are not vigilant, your ego can sneak in and dominate a situation before you even know it is there. Usually, you will find out too late when the chaos or conflict come to skuttle the goal being desired. If you are lucky and spiritually connected, at times you will hear the "still, small voice" warning you.

Let me give you an example regarding the writing of this book. Before this book was written, in my sleep I dreamt I was reading this book. That is how I knew it was time to write this book. I thought I was prayed up and conscious as I began to write. Remember I said, the ego can be a chameleon so whatever you want to achieve the ego can do that. As I wrote the first draft of this book, my ego was all over it! After three-hours, my ego said the main structure of the book was done in record time. I thought "Oh my God this is amazing." I must really be connected to my Spirit until I sat down to read a printed a copy. In the first draft of this book, it was railing against family and friends about how they did me wrong!

The book was horrible! It was a full-on rant of criticism and judgment about everybody but me. Let me give you a hint. The first indication that your ego is involved is when you are always talking about what somebody else needs to be doing instead of yourself! When you're operating from the Spirit, you know what needs to be done to benefit yourself as well as others. It's never about what somebody else needs because you are not trying to control their behavior to benefit yourself.

I went to sleep and upon waking the next day all I heard was, "You know your spiritualized-ego created that version of the book." No wonder it was so bad. I trashed that version and immediately started dictating an updated version of the book. After about an hour, when I looked up at the screen, it was blank! I was in shock and disbelief that not one word of what I said had been recorded. Instead of being mad, I laughed and then said to my ego, it doesn't matter because this book is already written and shall come into form. With that, I took a break and ate an ice cream sundae with caramel sauce before dictating this current version of the book.

Emotions Are Magnetic

Many people are not clear that emotions are enormously powerful and magnetic. If I had gotten upset about the initial version of this book, I can assure you this current version would never have been written. It is important to control your thoughts and your emotions but not by suppressing them. The trick is to fully express your authentic emotionality, so the ego has nothing to anchor itself to. This means you cannot be easily pulled off your center. It is from this place when we are more transparent that we can magnetize more positive situations.

If you are thinking a negative thought, you still magnetize it to you through your filters. In life, you can't get what you don't believe. If all you believe is something negative will happen, then in your theme park that is what you are going to experience. This is a self-fulfilling prophecy and the root of the "Law of Attraction."

As for me, I could attract almost anything, so manifestation was not my issue. Instead, my issue was holding the manifestation because one of my subconscious beliefs was "I am responsible for the behavior of others." As a result, if anybody (family, boyfriend, or girlfriend) stepped into my world after I had manifested something, but they needed something different, then my attention was immediately drained away collapsing my creation.

Subconscious Also Magnetizes

My subconscious conditioning reinforced everybody else was more important than myself. Given this belief, you can imagine the kind of rides I was taken on. It was easy to get me to do what people needed or wanted for all they had to do was "holler and scream" at me long enough or "guilt me through whining" then I would comply often responding with, "Ok, I'll help you." This was part of my subconscious conditioning which brought situations to me to fix reinforcing the distorted beliefs that "others are more important because I don't matter."

The new problem became once I agreed to "help" it often became my responsibility to do it! I would recommend something and help initially. But the person could not see the vision I had suggested needing more help until I was the only one helping. If I stopped at that moment, the problem I was called in to solve would have been worse than if I had not gotten involved in the first place. Now, I'm doubly mad because I'm way off of course for myself because I'm all caught up in somebody else's world. This amusement park ride is absolutely one I could have done without, not taken multiple times!

As part of the process of putting my "Ego on Front Street," I had to own and accept that I magnetized these crazy experiences to myself so I could be the "savior." What I know now but did not realize then was "help is not always helpful." In too many cases, I was initially being helpful for my own benefit, not theirs. This is the ultimate "spiritualized ego." Who am I to decide who needs help? Who am I to decide what kind of help they need? Who am I to decide what lessons a person can learn from a negative experience? Who am I to interfere with another's "personal sovereignty" especially since I do not understand how situations are universally designed to help others grow emotionally and spiritually? If there is some role for me to play, it must come out of the silence orchestrated by divine guidance otherwise my intentions are misguided.

I shared this to show that what we subconsciously believe affect us and others. So, if you're living a life that you are hating then you are holding on to some beliefs that are no longer serving you. Rather than yelling and screaming at the people outside of you who are creating the conflict, it's time for you to see what beliefs you are holding on to? What is the originating event that is magnetizing similar events to you to resolve?

Remember the trigger causing your reaction is "not" coming from the current events but often from past events maybe even something that happened to you in childhood. These unexpressed and unresolved emotions are showing up to be healed. Use what life is showing you to move your world in a new direction. Take advantage of being triggered to root out whatever old belief is holding you in place. The problem is this old belief is no longer serving you and is inappropriate as a coping mechanism. This is the source of why it creates so much chaos and conflict for you.

Chapter 8

That's Not True

Let's talk about what happens in those first seven years of life that serve as the blueprint for the remainder of a person's life unless they make a conscious effort to change it. The formation in these early years can be very detrimental to the way a person sees reality. As mentioned before, I felt loved as I came into a family with a mother, father, and two sisters. However, all of this changed by the time I was three years old when my father divorced my mother.

Due to early programming in which I felt loved by my father through hugs and kisses, that way of interacting left me vulnerable to other men when my father left. As a result of being used to physically being touched by my father, I was an easy sexual mark for men. Whereas I was looking for love from men, they saw me as a sexual target leaving me the victim of sexual assaults beginning at age 5. It was not just the incidents that were traumatizing, but the beliefs about men that came out of these encounters were equally devasting. I always dreamt of having an ideal relationship with a man because I remember what it felt like to be loved by my father. But I was unable to produce this ideal relationship for any length of time because of my underlying trust issues with men.

Early Beliefs About Men

My subconscious beliefs around relationships with men is that they are "loving, fun, but soon gone" so they cannot be trusted. I didn't even know I held this belief but seemed to have trouble bonding long-term with men. I didn't really know why, and I couldn't figure it out. The result is I never got married owing partly to the inability to unscramble this level of conditioning.

It wasn't until I took a class on science and spirituality that I understood the importance of the first seven years of brain development in children. Between ages 2-6, children are just like sponges as they operate in the "theta state" of imagination lacking the ability for critical or rational thinking. The professor emphasized children are just recording information about how to engage the world in the future. He went on to say that if you want to change some subconscious belief you were conditioned with during this time, you must change it the same way it was inputted. This means using repetition such as affirmations or change it in the subconscious by instilling new beliefs as you fall sleep.

Time to Change My Beliefs About Men

I thought about my trust issues with men, and I wanted to reprogram that in myself. I thought long and hard on what would be the best way to make that happen. Ok, I got it! I will sign up for an online dating service but "not" to find someone as much as to use it as a tool to reconcile the fundamental beliefs I had about men. I committed to being online for 30 days and every night before I went to sleep, I would scan the pictures of the men who had shown an interest in meeting or connecting with me. I would scan their pictures and say how much I appreciated them because they were: reliable, loving, kind, thoughtful, caring, supportive, strong, and protective. Also, I would say that "I'm grateful they are in my world" then I would go to sleep. Well, that seemed innocuous enough.

What was surprising to me was the first time I did this, within 20 minutes of falling asleep, I was sitting straight up in the bed yelling about how "that's not true"! Men are "not" reliable...they will leave you...

abandon you...they don't care! As I opened my eyes, I found myself looking around in the dark. I fell back asleep laughing as I thought, "wow, I've got work to do." This way of engaging went on for a while first reciting positive qualities about men, then falling asleep, only to be pulled out of a deep sleep yelling "that's not true"!

Unfortunately for me, I woke up every single night for almost two straight weeks objecting to a different quality every night. I always talked myself back to sleep by countering a negative experience with a positive one because many of my encounters with men were not always traumatizing. Finally, I could do the exercise of scanning the pictures and reciting these positive attributes of men then sleep soundly through the night. The effect on my outer world has been more help and support from men in the little activities of life such as holding doors or helping me with heavy items. I welcome support from men more easily now.

Letting Go of Daddy Issues

I shared this to say it is important we find ways to reprogram what has happened to us when we were children. It is not always so easy to make a change in our conscious minds then also think we are making a corresponding change in the core of who we are. We've got to find ways to "let go" of what makes us "mad and sad" on the inside. My father leaving made me mad and sad for a long time. Even though I interacted with him regularly after becoming an adult, I still felt resentment.

Now it was time to refocus my attention on the real problem that I had with "my daddy." I spent a lot of time in childhood trying "not" to be like him. As a result, I became "overly responsible" because I viewed him as "irresponsible" for leaving me. Another thing I did was I stayed in relationships longer than I needed to because I viewed him as "not" committed. I found myself doing the exact opposite of things I wanted to do just because I didn't want to be like him! The real problem is because I am "half him" yet I am fighting against that half of myself that is him. This war within me raged for decades until life coaching skills allowed me to finally reconcile that "I am like him;" I needed to own those perceived negative qualities in myself.

If I am honest with myself there are times when I need to be "non-committed" especially when others are not doing their part. There are times when I need to be "irresponsible." As I started accepting those qualities in myself it was amazing how much more

59

love, I could begin to feel for myself and for him. Then the realization hit me like a ton of bricks that it was time to forgive him for leaving me at three years old.

Never Too Late to Grieve

From time to time, I asked my father why he left, so I did have some information about what was going on in his life at the time. At the point he divorced my mother, my father was in his early twenties. He said the pressure became too much as he was dealing with the death of his father as well as the death his best friend from childhood. As I pressed him about why he didn't stay or take me, he admitted something I always felt. He said to me, "You were just a pawn in the game." Rather than be mad or angry about that statement, it confirmed what I felt. I responded to him that I knew he loved me but at the time he left, I felt that "I didn't matter."

My father died a decade ago, but I have often thought about my conversations with him. I was grateful to have finally found the point of origination of the theme to my life that "I don't matter," it came from my father leaving me at age 3. What I also realized was that when he left, I never had a chance to grieve him especially since nobody talks to a 3-year-old about her emotions. To have somebody who loves, hugs, and kisses you to be suddenly gone is like a death. With this realization, late one night I allowed that 3-year-old part of myself to grieve. Oh my God, the tears that flowed were unbelievable.

For the first time, I could finally feel my own emotional body and it felt free. How many of us have deep seated childhood wounds that we have not grieved? How many of us have not allowed our hearts to break from the pain we truly feel? What I found fascinating was once I felt heard and expressed in terms of my grief then I asked a question that I had never thought about before. All my life, I have always focused on the question "What about me?"

Now with regards to my father, the question is "Where is your compassion for him for what he was going through that made him leave?" At that moment, I cried all over again because for the first time I was now able to see beyond the sight of a 3-year-old. I was now able to see and feel somebody else's pain. This also made me more aware of my mother's pain and cried even harder. I grieved for all of us that night.

When I finally went to sleep for the first time ever, I could now see beyond myself. The ride at my theme park of "I don't matter" had come to an end. I am the one who kept that belief in play because I never acknowledged the point of origination in which my emotions got stuck. I spent a lifetime magnetizing to myself situations that always had me asking, "What about me"? Going back to the point of origination to retrieve my own emotions has interrupted this pattern and is what is allowing me to consider the emotions of others.

Chapter 9

Never Too Late

As many of you know, the ego does not see itself as wrong therefore it is not trying to apologize. Let's get that straight. So, if you're trying to get someone else to apologize first who has a strong ego, let me save you the trouble, they will not do it! How is forgiveness possible? Therein lies our dilemma. This may also explain why there is so much unhappiness in the world because so many people are waiting for others to make the first move. "I'm not going to apologize to her; she should apologize to me since it was her fault." If you then talk to the other person, they will tell you the same thing. "I'm not going to apologize to her; she should apologize to me it was her fault."

There is too much of "us vs. them" going on in society as people are caught in the grips of their egos. Forgiveness is the way to see a little crack in the door that allows you to begin to detach yourself from your own ego. For it is only in the forgiveness process that you can begin to own your "contribution to the chaos ". Once you are free to admit to yourself that you were wrong then ideas may now come to you which will allow you to make amends or atone for the breach in the relationship. Remember, it's never too late to offer forgiveness.

The Fight is On

The ego's grip on ourselves begins to loosen the moment we admit that we were wrong. We are now free to see things in totality. The problem with living from the ego's perspective is that we only see just a slice of reality, never really tuning in to another person's worldview. There is a tendency to go through life seeing through filters or sunglasses which selectively edit out anything that does not agree with our point of view. This belief or philosophy will always create conflict with others when they are not seeing things exactly as we do. And, of course, there is only one "right" way to think about anything according to the ego.

Under the guidance of the ego, instead of us opening our minds and hearts to see how we can communicate more effectively, we become defensive and aggressive with those who see life through a different lens. That defensiveness and aggressiveness is what can also trigger the other person. Depending on the filters through which they see their reality, then the fight is on! How do we de-escalate the tension? How do we bring conflict to an end?

One More Step

One of the most effective ways to de-escalate conflict is through the process of forgiveness. I am not talking about "forgiveness lite" meaning a quick fast in a hurry type of forgiveness where you say, "I forgive you so let's move on" without dealing with the underlying issues that created the conflict and emotional pain in the first place. To be whole and complete, you must be able to take the relationship back to its point of origination before the arguments began which broke it down. If you have truly forgiven someone then you have repaired the relationship in such a way as to function like the argument never happened. You will share and care for one another like old times. If you cannot do that then know you have not reached a point of "true forgiveness" and more work is needed.

The real challenge is taking one more step to resolve a situation. Sometimes the only way out is through which may mean additional discussions over your perceptions of their wrongdoing. Why is it so hard for some of us to say, "I have a problem with what you did" or "I need you to explain your thought process"? Why can't we have discussions after arguments from a place of neutrality instead of a place of anger and belligerence? Coming at people like that only makes them defensive, sparking a new round of arguments. There will always be differences of opinion because we each prioritize variables differently that go into our decision-making process.

The main reason there is conflict is that neither party is open to "divine or intuitive guidance" which often allows a decision to be made from a place of higher consciousness which then benefits everyone. If we are willing to open ourselves up to hear, see, and understand the opposition in a whole new way, then we can make tremendous gains on our road toward living in oneness with one another.

Life Coaching to the Rescue

Let me give you an example of what operating in this way could potentially look like. As mentioned before, I have been a life coach for almost 20 years now. During that time, I have had professors and clients who have brought me new information about how I function as well as the restrictions on how I see reality. In turn, I have brought a lot of these coaching concepts to my family as we have had our own share of struggles. Given that we are all life-long learners, we have tried to incorporate various aspects of these techniques into how we engage with one another.

Recently, I participated in a global workshop on the topic of mothers and daughters looking at their patterns of engagement. A question came up about how relationships change as daughters move into adulthood. My mother who was also participating in the global zoom call, answered the question stating that it is the daughter who should established the new ways of interacting. I in turn was asked the same question to get a daughter's perspective.

After some hesitation, I responded that it was "not" always possible for the daughter to make changes to the relationship because in my case, "I was brought up to fear my mother who was the final authority." To me this meant there was a limit on my self- expression if my opinion differed from hers. I was brought up to go only so far in an argument. The goal of parents was to instill discipline and respect for authority because parents believed in "spare the rod, spoil the child."

Robin L. Johnson

PTSD Through Conditioning

Although not intentional on her part, fearing my mother's temper went on for many years during my youth. The conditioning became a pattern that was not so easily broken just because I became an adult. For me even as an adult, you could imagine my "Post Traumatic Stress Disorder" (PTSD) if I had to have a disagreement with my mother or anybody in authority for that matter. It took all I had to just speak up sometimes in a quivering voice but always with an eye on shutting down immediately if the one in authority responded aggressively. I was conditioned "not" to fully express what I was feeling because when the PTSD was triggered in me, I believed if I went farther, there was the possibility I could be physically hit. Only when I experienced rage, my anger overcame the fear, then I would respond in an aggressive manner towards those in authority not caring about their reaction.

After that workshop, it led to a dynamic conversation between me and my mother. She was surprised to learn how I still saw her through the "eyes of a child" even though I was an adult. I told her, you never came back to me as an adult and said, "You are free to have your opinions without worrying about me potentially hitting you." So, she made that declaration to me immediately. What a beautiful gift I received that day. Even though it was decades in the making, I cannot begin to tell you how freeing a conversation that was for me and my mother. Parents are not always conscious of the impact of their behaviors on their children and can't always imagine how basic discipline could be distorted in a child's mind.

Walk in Someone's Shoes

Few people will debate the idea that we can all use some doses of "oneness and harmony." How do you bring harmony to your world? Who is it in your world that you need to resolve issues with? Unfortunately, too many people on the spiritual path have ready-made answers to resist solving conflict. Phrases used include: "Oh that's in the past, just leave it there... I'm not dealing with that anymore...I already have tried once before and I'm not going to try anymore...I already know what they think." Do you really know what they think? Do you really understand how they saw their reality that contributed to the conflict? If the answer is "Yes," then you would not have a problem freely engaging with them again.

More of an effort needs to be made to understand what it feels like to walk in someone else's shoes. Are we willing to try and understand someone else's story? Unfortunately, too many of us on a spiritual path profess to "love God" who we can't see but won't love our brothers and sisters who we see every day. How can we profess to be spiritual if we won't even do the basic thing and try to love one another? If you are serious about moving forward with your spiritual journey and experiencing "partnership with God," efforts need to be made to let go of the anger you are harboring against others. You must reconcile your situations before full "partnership with God" is possible because this kind of negative emotional baggage will never allow you to surrender your own personal agenda in favor of God's will.

Chapter 10

Hide and Seek

People have asked, "How do we make changes in our lives that are permanent?" I always suggest beginning with being authentic in answering the following questions. Why do you want to make this change? Who benefits if you make this change? Who loses if you make this change? These questions are important because they create the roadmap for where you want to go. If you are not committed to making changes in your life for the right reasons, then you will quit when the road gets difficult.

The path to uncover where your ego is hiding is a challenge, but attachment to the ego needs to be dissolved if permanent changes are to be made in your life. It is not always easy to identify why your ego is driving your behavior by making self-sabotaging decisions that are not in your best interest. The answers you uncover may require you to let go of something or someone you value. If you don't let go, your ego can find a place to hide in the dissatisfaction.

Where is the ego is hiding? The answer to that question is simple. Ego hides everywhere in your life where you have secrets and unexpressed negative emotionality. So rather than deal with the inner turmoil, the ego projects it out resulting in conflict. Remember the purpose of the ego is to keep you separate and isolated, so nobody gets close enough to create hurt, harm, or danger. What better way to do this than through constant confrontation? Beware of people who say, that is just my personality, or this is just the way I am. That may be true, but if you look deeper, you may find their ego hiding behind walls of emotional pain.

Confrontation is a Clue

One of the easiest ways to spot ego is through constant confrontation. Just because I have a difference of opinion from you doesn't mean our discussion has to end in conflict. There is no need to confront someone because they have a unique perspective on the same topic. But the ego believes its perspective is the only "right answer" and argue with others trying to convince them of this. We each must come to the realization that we only see a slice of reality. No one person has a monopoly on the "right answer" in matters of opinion in the world of subjective human thought. Each person should be free to think and see reality as they wish.

To begin the process of identifying where your ego hides, you must start by being honest with yourself, be authentic, acknowledge that "you are not all that." When you can own your faults and your frailties, then you are well down the road to healing your broken heart. It is from this place that you can stop projecting your unhealed feelings onto others. In reining in your ego, an important thing to remember is that your ego is easily identified through the "triggers." It's those events that cause you or the person you are interacting with to react with anger, hostility, defensiveness, or belligerence.

Triggers are coming from the filters through which you see your reality. Remember those filters are coming from your conditioning, background, culture, education, and experience. The things that trigger you are not necessarily the same things that will trigger someone else. Triggers indicate limitation because you see your reality a certain way causing another person's reality to clash with yours. You are not allowing for any other thoughts than your own.

When you do that then you limit how you see reality because we evolve only when we allow the opinions of others to help us shift our perspectives.

Only My Opinion Matters

Everyone's opinion is valid, but the problem comes when the ego is in positions of authority and uses its authority to dominate and control opposition thoughts. This is when it's dangerous because when you begin to limit oppositional thoughts rather than include them, you begin to stagnate the development of humanity. No one should have the right to take away someone else's rights simply because they see things differently. It is in the variety that we are all able to grow together. There is validity in all perspectives because you must remember that what you are sharing is just one slice of reality based on your experience.

At what point do we all realize that one individual does not have all the answers for everybody else. When do you realize just because you see it differently it doesn't make you right? When do you acknowledge that just because you are triggered, that it's not someone else's fault? Not understanding these concepts is what continues to get us in trouble and allows our ego to continue to hide.

Ego is Really a Coward

As you identify areas of confrontation where your ego is hiding, you must be understanding and compassionate with yourself. This makes the process of putting your "Ego on Front Street" a little easier. It's interesting that once you expose your ego around a certain issue or topic then your ego tends not to return to defend that issue. If you are arguing with someone about something but you release your defensiveness and aggression, claiming you were wrong, then your perception shifts. If you can "own your contribution to the chaos" admitting you misperceived the issue, then your ego tends to find a different place to hide.

The ego does not tend to come back to those same issues you surrendered to continue to fight for domination. You see, the ego is somewhat of a coward. It will argue but it needs to be hidden in that argument. Ironically, once the ego is exposed it loses energy. The strength of the ego comes from the darkness where it hides while it fuels conflict and chaos from its well of negative emotions. Once you step into the light and understand why you see reality the way you do, then the ego loses control over you. It is at this point that the attachment to tangible physical reality gives way to the infinite invisible reality of God.

Chapter 11

God is Like Steam

There is so much more to us than just our "ego-self" for we are not giving nearly enough airtime to our "divine-self" where we experience spontaneous right actions and synchronicities. Life becomes like magic, as what we need, just magically appears. The driver for this way of being is in the heart rather than in the mind. That is why my life coaching mentor Debbie Ford would often say, "the longest journey you will ever take is the one from your head to your heart."

What does it mean to live from your heart and follow the divine impulses? Who and what is God? There are as many answers to these questions as there are people on the planet. No one answer is the right answer. This is one of the reasons why we have so many religions and denominations within religions. But despite the differences, 85% of the people in the world, according to the 2020 census, still believe in God as the creator of life on earth.

Essential Essence of Man

Although I have traveled to over forty countries and studied most of the world's major religions, by choice and training, I am a Christian. I do not adhere to everything in the Christian doctrine, but I am a devoted follower of Jesus Christ's spiritual philosophy to "act justly, love mercy and walk humbly with God."

My biggest struggle has been finding a process which can help me minimize my ego-self while maximizing my divine-self to live life from a place of balance and equanimity. I always believed it was possible to be "in it and not of it." Learning to follow intuitive or divine guidance is essential in this way of being. I remember struggling with the concept of "Who and What God was to me?"

One day while meditating in my apartment in Washington D.C., I asked, "What does it mean that man is made in the image of God?" This question arose because of some reading I was doing in the Holy Bible. In response I could hear the "still small voice" of my Spirit reply, "go make a cup of tea." What? How is that going to answer my question, I thought to myself? As I had gotten used to doing, I followed the divine guidance even though it made no sense. I got up, went to the kitchen to put the tea pot on the stove. As the water started to boil, I could see steam coming out. It was then I heard, "that is the image of God." Oh snap! I got it right away. Man, who is made in the image of God, has nothing to do with our physical bodies. If you needed to make it visual, then the "essential essence" that animates our bodies is like "steam"!

I was then guided to try to capture the steam. It was very illusive. I swung my arms wildly through the air trying to capture the steam. I tried containing it by wrapping my arms around it, but it slipped around my arms. I tried holding it down with my hands on top but that too failed as steam slipped through my fingers. Nothing I did would allow me to capture the steam with my bare hands. At this point, I was laughing hysterically. What a profound concept? The "essential essence" of man is like steam.

Did I Really Get Hurt?

As I continued to ponder this new idea, I started to take it a bit further. If it is true that "man is made in the image of God" and if this image is "more like steam" than it is a physical body, then how can you say that anything that has happened to me in my life could have hurt me? Think about the profound implications of this for all the emotional damage I held onto from verbal, physical and sexual abuse. Yes, those things really happened but to my physical body, not to the "essential essence" of who God created me to be.

From this perspective, all the abuse we talk about in society focuses on the physical body and the possessions that support the body. However, the "essential essence" of who you are is steam and is "not" accessible by others outside of the body. That's something to think. In these terms that makes man unassailable and invulnerable. Now I can understand how Jesus Christ after been beaten and hung on a cross could say, "Forgive them Father for they know not what they do." I also understand how the most outrageous and egregious acts committed by man can be forgiven by those truly deep into their spirituality.

It we take this concept out to its logical conclusion, then nothing anybody has ever done to you requires you to respond with anger or hostility. So, it should be easy, not hard, to offer true forgiveness as you "turn the other cheek" or "love your enemies." There is nothing anybody can do to hurt you. Even if they killed you, they could only kill off your physical body, so the essential essence of you that God created would still exist. I don't know about you, but I love this idea that the essential essence of me is like steam because that makes me "untouchable"!

Paying the Price

You know everyone has a spiritual philosophy, but the true test is "Can you live what you say you believe?" Most of us are unwilling to pay the price for what we say we want. As for me, I wanted to actualize this spiritual philosophy. I wanted to be so connected to my divine guidance that I could handle anything. I wanted to face challenges in my life, remembering that "I am steam"! Great philosophy, but what happens if living in this new reality cost you everything in your tangible physical reality. Would you pay the price? As Jesus asked his disciples, "Will you give up everything and follow me"? I did…

Over a decade ago, I remember coming home from work one day thinking to myself, "I am sitting on top of the world"! I recently secured a $2 million contract billing the U.S. government $70,000 per month to pay subcontractors and employees. I am flying around the world first class staying in whatever five-star hotel I felt like. I was "living the dream" but found no joy in it once attained. What is wrong with me? How can this be true? Nobody prepared me for the emptiness that could come with success.

In my distressed state, I cried out, "God it doesn't feel like you are in any of what I'm doing." All I heard was "alright then, give it up!" My response was "Ok, not a problem" because my spiritualized ego convinced me I would have all this back in no time. Little did I know giving up everything to follow God would require me to change my values. The slide off the mountain top of financial success into the ocean of the "financial shark tank" of debt collectors was almost immediate. Gone were the symbols of my "tangible success" such as my house in suburban Philadelphia, my BMW shipped in from Germany, and my jewelry bought from countries around the world.

I Did Not Sign Up for This

In short order, I lost everything I valued! The only thing I had left was my spiritual philosophy which was hanging by a thread. At this point, this God in whom I had trusted, I was telling off regularly with some choice language I might add. "God, wake up… Are you sleep up there? … My life is falling apart, do something! … I did not sign up for this!" But given time, since I could not change anything, I settled in to this new "minimalist lifestyle." I began to see how my entire value system was being restructured. Gone were the days of speeding around in my BMW or flying first-class or even flying at all!

A new introspection took over. I could clearly see my ego at work in my previous life. I saw how I accomplished material goals but at what price. I was beginning to see how my ego-self had guided and directed everything. Soon I realized everything I did in support of others was done with me knowing in advance how this was going to benefit me. This revelation was jarring because I viewed myself as the "spiritual one" who did for others under the "guise of altruism." Now my ability to engage with the world in my usual superficial way was taken away.

After 30 years of living alone in other cities, I was now engaging with my family of origin. I lost my house but was able to sell it a week before foreclosure and use the profits to build a studio apartment connected to a family member's house. What was stunning to me was when I started to engage with my family again, it was like no time had passed. The old patterns I did "not" like growing up came roaring back forcing me to confront even more of my subconscious beliefs that I thought I had handled. Nothing like family to help you deal with your issues.

I knew what I was looking at and why I was back. Issues were coming up for healing to free myself from my distorted belief system. Nothing that happens to us in life is wasted because everything that happens to us serves a purpose on the road to enlightenment. The question is, "Can we take advantage of what we are being shown to make the changes required from the inside?"

Another Way to Live

When I think back on over my life, I am grateful for the experiences I have had. I am also clear about the choices I made to advance my spiritual development. More than ever, I am convinced there is more to life than striving, planning, scheming, and organizing every day to make something happen. When I was living like that, I found it exhausting. There must be another way to live life.

Recently I came across one of my favorite books called the "Thunder of Silence" by Joel Goldsmith. In it, he talks about how in the human scene the mind is creative as it creates both good and evil. He goes on to say that mind in this spiritual scene is "not" creative but an "avenue of awareness" ready to follow the "divine impulses." The difference he says is like having a canvas and instead of you racking your brain trying to figure out what to paint, you step back asking the Spirit of God within "to paint what you will."

According to the author, in this new way of living, if we can create space then we can give the Spirit of God room to step in and help guide us. The goal on the spiritual journey is to have a partnership with God in "constructive creation" in a way that benefits the whole including the self. This way of being is not about doing something "for God" as much as it is about doing something "with God."

Chapter 12

Charcoal to Diamonds

As I have said before, many of the beliefs that we have originate in our childhood. If we could only go back in time and bring forth the "inner child" to make that person feel "safe" and "truly loved," then we could really transform ourselves. Rather than healing ourselves from within, many of us react to life's pressure on a continuum from charcoal to diamonds. Some of us tend to react in a combustible fashion like charcoal while others use the pressure to transform into diamonds. Rather you are combustible like charcoal, or you are strong like diamonds depends on your reaction to pressure.

Stuck in 3D

Experiences are colored by the filters through which we see our reality. As has been said before, it is life's early experiences that become the default programming

85

for our behavior. The bigger problem is that we do not stop and shed that original programming which no longer serves us. We know when we experience the end of the usefulness of a belief because continuing to employ that belief or way of being, creates conflict and chaos.

It is this original programming which holds us in three-dimensional (3D) reality where we are limited to our five senses to determine what is real and what is false. We use our intellect to analyze and synthesize the data that comes in from our five senses to make decisions. The conclusions we reach are based upon previous experiences and standards that come out of our default map created when we were children. Most of us have outgrown that way of being. We have outgrown the old standards and useless data that fill up our minds. As a result, we are highly combustible like charcoal because we are not getting the results we want from our decision-making. We are stuck. We are limited.

How do we move from our 3D view of reality? How do we transform into diamonds under pressure? Is it possible to see reality in such a way as to be "responsive" rather than "reactive"? To get to this new way of being, most of us need to unpack our emotional baggage which means to deal with our broken hearts.

Too many of us have compartmentalized the traumas and dramas of life. We are "not" allowing ourselves to truly feel what we feel. Our hearts have become obstacle courses through which we are trying to navigate to experience the fullness of life.

What if we realized we had the power to redesign the obstacle course? What if we could take out the obstacles that we put there in the first place? What if we could be transformed from charcoal to diamonds? Simply put, if we make one major change to our thought process then the obstacle course as we know it could disappear.

Law of Attraction

The change we need to make has to do with the Law of Attraction. At some time in our lives, we all have made promises that we "would not let certain things happen to us again." In making this statement, we have now set in motion the "Law of Attraction." As we try hard "not" to let negative things happen to us again, we are actually magnetizing those experiences to us through the law of attraction. You see, you get what you think about even if those thoughts are negative.

Let me give you an example. I had a fundamental belief in "harmony" at all costs. When I looked further as to why I carried this belief, I could see it was a by-product of childhood trauma. Way into my adulthood, I was always trying to keep people around me harmonious by intervening to stop any arguments. I was all too willing to trade my "happiness" for "peace." In taking a hard look at why I behaved in such a manner. It was finally revealed to me. I realized I never felt "safe" in environments where people were arguing.

As I took the time to review my own childhood, I could see the origins of this distorted belief. In my 3-year-old mind, it was arguments that lead to permanent separation because this was the age at which my parents were divorced. After that separation, I began to associate arguments with physical punishment. If I disagreed with those in authority, the result was too often a spanking.

Not understanding the degree to which these experiences infiltrated my consciousness, as an adult, I did not or could not accept any relationship that brought forward intense arguments because I believed people who were out of control put my safety at risk. The problem is this outdated belief that arguments lead to me being "unsafe" was no longer true. However, that did not stop my subconscious belief, thereby activating the law of attraction. So, what did I attract into my adulthood, lots of situations in which people were emotionally out of control and occasions in which I got hit!

Time to Change the Channel

My perception, based upon my experiences, created a default program that was no longer serving me. It was time to change the channel. Many of us want to have transformation happen without releasing or letting go of those negative emotions that are holding us in our heart space. As a life coach, to change the channel on some past conditioning, I would often let myself react authentically. After the conflict was over, I would then start the analysis. What is this situation reminding me of? How old is my inner child who is reacting to this situation? Who did this to me before? Who made me feel badly in a similar situation? Who left me feeling victimized? As I began to answer those questions within myself, then I was able to release some of the old beliefs.

For me personally, since I am a writer, I would use journaling as my process for release. I would first identify a current conflict, then pretend that I was back in time. I would identify my inner child who was reacting who was usually between the ages 3 to 9 years old. That was often the age range where the originating painful event was found. I would write about how I felt about the current event then take myself back to the first time or the originating event that was never fully addressed. I would allow myself to freely address the person in authority. I imagined "Little Robin" having the power to tell off those in authority who were creating a problem for me.

I was often surprised at the freedom that came from truly expressing on paper how I felt giving voice to what I would no longer tolerate from someone. This dialogue allowed my heart to release some negative emotions that were stuck there. Once I could do that in writing then I was able to begin the forgiveness process of the person involved in the current situation. But there is no forgiveness possible if your heart is unhealed. Many of us want to forgive people, but we are still mad at them for what they have done.

New Priority

It is hard to have permanent transformation when you are unwilling to make yourself your own priority. You say you desire to transform yourself, but your full attention is external. To become the diamond, you are truly meant to be, you must be willing to take the "inner journey." Time to see what is holding you back and what outdated beliefs are no longer serving you. The childhood conditioning must be released since we're no longer children powerless to control our reality.

Yet, we're trying to hold ourselves in the same outdated belief systems which hold us in 3D causing so much anger, resentment, frustration, and violence. There must be a way to release ourselves from that level of pressure because not doing so leaves us combustible like charcoal.

Chapter 13

Stepping Out of the Box

It is time to step out of this limited way of thinking by stepping out-of-the-box. It is time to step into a higher level of consciousness of oneness, cooperation, synchronicity, spontaneous right actions, support, love, joy, and happiness. It is time to step into the fifth dimension (5D) where everything is effortless and harmonious for self and others. Gone is the playground of the ego which chaos, conflict, and separation reign as the hallmark of 3D reality.

Stepping freely into 5D reality means your open heart allows for divine guidance to navigate your new reality. All your past pain from trauma and drama has been fully acknowledged, expressed, and let go. None of what has happened to you in 3D can be taken with you into 5D reality. "Connectivity" is the name of the game in 5D. Everybody's interest is also yours and your interest is now everybody else's. There is no way of being that separates you from another person.

The good news is you now have let go of your emotional baggage, so you no longer fear others. Gone are the days of shielding yourself from hurt, harm or danger. In 5D, you live and embrace the concept that the essential essence of who you are is like "steam" not the physical body you see in the mirror.

Children Run 3D

Seeing the essential essence of yourself as steam makes it impossible for anybody to victimize you because they can't control you. If we stay in alignment with God, we have dominion over all forces in 3D reality. What makes something real is you feeding your emotional energy into it, giving it power. As you let go of the 3D reality, there is no thought of danger. Instead, you begin to see those still operating in 3D as children. Do you honestly believe that a 3-, 4-, or 5-year-old can seriously hurt you as an adult?

As you watch people operating in 3D reality, instead of fear, you begin to see the "games people play". You easily ask yourself questions like: Are you kidding me? Do you really think you are going to get away with that? I see everything you are doing just like parents see the behavior of their children. It is easy and effortless in 5D to see the intentions and motivations as people are in the planning stages. Remember, you are fully connected to everyone, and it becomes easy to sense their motivations.

From your new perspective in 5D reality, the biggest thing that happens is you now have compassion instead of anger for someone trying to create hurt, harm, or danger. You understand it is their outdated belief system operating which causes them to be stuck in past patterns. There is no way that somebody who is stuck in a 3D childhood pattern can have a negative impact on someone with a higher level 5D of consciousness. It is just an impossibility.

Flowing in 5D

As you move into this 5D reality, it is really a wonderful way to live because the synchronicity and flow are amazing. You easily see the connectivity of all things which bring much joy and happiness to your relationships. Since I have stepped more fully into this 5D reality, I have become far more tolerant. I freely interact with people long enough to find out more about our inter-connectivity. Before I would easily get agitated with others trying to figure out why beyond a certain point, people were still engaging with me. Now what happens is, as I'm having a conversation with family, friends, or even strangers sometimes I stay engaged long enough to find out something we have in common where we can mutually support each other. This is very magical because I am not anticipating this going into any conversation.

Let me give you an example from my own life. I was having a casual conversation with my relative about her taking care of her great niece (5) and nephew (3). We were talking about the kind of day they had and as we finished that conversation we keep talking. As we continued talking, she mentioned she needed a ride to run some errands. Since I was free and available in that moment, I offered to take her. Within an hour, she had done everything she needed to do and was very happy. There was no motivation for me taking her other than it was to be helpful to her, but the result is my relative treated me to dinner for helping her. This is 5D reality at it best. No hidden agendas for serving others.

The same can be said for another encounter with another relative. As I was talking to her, she mentioned she wanted to take her grandchildren to the "Night-Out" celebration at our local mall. It has become a big event in our community, where families come together with their children to learn about services including interacting with firefighters and policemen.

I just happen to ask her who was going with her and her grandchildren. To my surprise she responded, "Nobody but I think I'd like to take them." I volunteered to go with her. She was grateful as the kids were highly active and animated. Moving around the celebration, it became apparent it took both of us to keep up with the little ones fascinated by everything. We all had an enjoyable time on a beautiful summer evening in August.

Mutually Beneficial

As you begin to move into 5D reality you will find you are often where you need to be. Spontaneous right actions and synchronicity tend to be the norm producing results that benefit everybody. I like to say to people that standard operating procedure in 5D is "everything is mutually beneficial". I have no hesitation about saying to people in 3D, "if it only benefits you, don't call me"! It is like if I am going north and you're going north then by all means let's go together. However, if I am going north and you're going south, then we must go our separate ways. I now know I will eventually feel anger and resentment if I stop going north just to help you go south where the only benefit is to you. I am no longer willing to live from this place of lack and limitation feeding my ego blame and grievance.

It feels so much better to operate in way that is mutually beneficial having outcomes that benefit the whole. It's only 3D reality where people will tell you, "I need your help" but refuse to help you. It's only 3D reality when people want to use your time, your money, and your resources exclusively for their benefit with no thought about how to help you. In 5D reality, you don't even give thought to doing something that only benefits yourself without a corresponding benefit to those who will be affected. This is where we need to go individually. This is where we need to go in families. This is where we need to go in our communities. This is where we need to go in our country. This is where we need to go in our world. We must move to this higher level of consciousness where the needs of the whole are always considered.

Chapter 14

Dissolving the Ego's Attachment

Many of us want to live our lives with more love and more flow. For the divine energy to move easily through you, it requires you to heal your heart because that is the anchoring point for the Divine. Are there people you still hate? Are there people with whom you are still mad? Are there people you have not forgiven? Are there people about whom you are still complaining? Are you still carrying secrets? Do you have work to do to heal your broken heart? If you answered "Yes" to any of these questions, then you have work to do to become a "clear channel" as your spiritual awakening is still in progress.

The main thing that keeps us anchored in 3D reality is our ego. This book is about recognizing the influence of your ego and exposing it by putting it on Front Street. It is only in 3D reality that your ego is free to dominate. In 5D reality, the attachment to the ego gets "dissolved" as you are now being led by the Divine.

Recognizing Emotional Boomerangs

How do you dissolve your attachment to your ego? Many concepts have been talked about in this book, but the primary gateway is by healing your heart because the ego got created from that wounded place within you. Another important thing to do is to rescue your inner child who got caught in the trauma. Once you do this, it will create enough separation to allow you to see the ego's behavior in action. You can easily recognize when your ego is throwing out a boomerang to create chaos or conflict and then you can stop reacting to it. Remember, the purpose of your ego is to keep you safe, and it does this by keeping your separate.

In this context, "emotional boomerang" is some aspect of your behavior that is unknowingly thrown out but then comes back to you. But since you cannot see your own behavior, you react as the victim. Too often we cannot see what beliefs lie deep within. Rather than take responsibility for our "contribution to the chaos," we begin the process of blaming others for the results. We never see how what we said or what we did was the initial reason for another person's reaction. It might be something as simple as doing things that someone has told us irritates them or criticizing another. Sometimes it might mean being aggressive or belligerent when the situation does not call for that. All of these scenarios are a result of throwing out boomerangs.

This ego process of throwing out boomerangs then proclaiming its innocence must be interrupted. Whatever is happening in your life, you are the architect of the chaos coming into your life because you are the one allowing it. When we are operating from a higher consciousness, we are not in conflict with others because we are not in conflict with ourselves. We are often aware of the feelings of another person therefore if they react negatively to something we say or do, it is quickly met with apology or understanding from us, not defensiveness and aggression.

If you are trying to leave 3D reality permanently then you must continue to work on you. Stop feeding your ego with conflict and chaos which the ego thrives upon. Remember, the ego protects you by creating chaos and conflict which then separates you from others. It is in that separation where the ego perceives it is keeping you safe. Unfortunately, people are social beings, so isolation is never the desired outcome.

The ego's mechanism to keep us safe is by creating so much chaos and conflict that we tend to pull back. In that separation, it blames everybody else but itself. At some point, as you become aware of this pattern, you will say to your ego "enough is enough." I cannot continue to follow you in this self-sabotaging way of being.

Enlightenment in the Jacuzzi

When you no longer desire to follow your ego, do not be surprised at having a confrontation with it. Let me share my story about how I finally detached from my ego. I was having a really wonderful day hanging out in the 5D reality where everything was synchronistic. I was feeling so good that at the end of my day, I decided to jump into my jacuzzi tub. I ran the water temperature to just the right level of hot, then put in some coconut bath salts with a touch of frankincense oil from Egypt as I lit the candelabra.

As I stepped into the jacuzzi tub, I am loving my life in that moment sharing gratitude in my conversations with God. Since I am clairsentient, I hear the voice of the Divine very clearly. I thanked God for all that was done for me that day and for the way my life was turning out. I also asked the question, "What else do I need to do to stay in this connection full time?" The answer that came back surprised me. I heard, "You need to put your ego out of your heart"! What? I thought I had already done that. Ok, no problem, that's easy.

I took a big deep breath then focused my attention on my heart. I started pushing and pushing when suddenly I heard a voice say, "Stop…Stop What are you doing?" I sat straight up in the tub and listened. It was like an out of body experience as this voice started saying to me, "You can't get rid of me." I responded by saying, "What do you mean I can't get rid of you"? The answer came back, "I'm your ego and I've always been here protecting you as it laughed in a deep growling voice." My reply, "I no longer need you because I'm following the Divine now, so I don't need you anymore."

To my surprise the voice of my ego started listing all the ways it was helpful to me. Remember when I helped you when you had a problem with this or that person? Remember when this person borrowed money and never paid it back? I listened as my ego recited how it helped me over the years. When it finished talking, I said "All of the things you have listed left me on the short end of the stick and mad with people. You were always self-sabotaging me. At no time when you were leading was, I successful in my dealings with anyone. You created chaos and conflict which made me withdraw because I couldn't stand the interaction anymore. I was always the loser following you. I lost money, lost friendships, lost my house, lost my jewelry, lost my car, lost everything following your leadership. So 'No,' I don't think I want to follow you anymore!"

The response from my ego was, "I have set-up shop in your heart when you were wounded and I'm never leaving." I thought to myself, we'll see about that. Unconsciously, I started EFT tapping with two fingers on meridian points in my face. Eventually, two fingers became three fingers then three fingers became open palms. I found myself banging on my chest like King Kong all the while saying, "If you are in charge, then stop me." I took my open palms then started smacking myself in the face while still yelling, "Stop me"!

My ego continued to demand, "Stop it, you're hurting me…Stop it." My response as I continued to hit myself was, "I am not hurting me because the essential essence of me is like steam, not this body… You make me stop, remember you said you have control over me." I continued smacking myself upside the head and pounding on my chest all the while laughing hysterically. Suddenly, it got really quiet, so I stopped. My mind was quiet, my body felt very calm. It was in that moment that I asked my ego, "Where are you"? With a faint voice, I heard my ego respond, "I cannot stay attached to anyone who does not value the body."

I share this story to point out a truth shared during this moment of enlightenment in the jacuzzi. What keeps our egos attached to us is our valuing of the body over the spirit that animates the body. When we can begin the process of detaching from "tanphys" (tangible/physical) reality in favor of embracing the spiritual reality, then we will be less resistant and more accepting of everything that is happening to us. We will know deep in our hearts that everything that is happening is for our greater good.

I can honestly say since the hot tub experience, I have not had any situation where I have been on the "short end of the stick" activating in me the need to holler, scream, or yell at somebody. Dissolving the bonds between me and my ego meant leaving 3D reality behind in favor of 5D reality. Using my multi-dimensional senses allows me to easily and effortlessly get my daily needs met.

Chapter 15

Ascension to 5D

We must end the reign of the ego where "individuality" dominates at the cost of the "collective." Too many people are running around talking about "I got mine" …" I don't care about you." There is no way we can survive as a society, if this is how we continue to operate with one another. This "way of being" must come to an end or it will devolve into complete chaos and anarchy. It is time to transcend this way of being. It is time to become who we were meant to be. I am calling on all to spiritually awaken, to open their heart space, to elevate their consciousness and to embrace ascension into the fifth dimension (5D). This change starts within yourself first. As is often quoted by Gandhi, "You must be the change you want to see in the world."

On this inner journey, don't worry about who knows, who cares, or who understands. Just stay authentic in your knowledge that how you are feeling needs to change. Be willing go and get your "inner child" who is stuck within you. Show that part of you some mercy. Show it some love. Show it some tenderness. Build it up and integrate it back into who you are. As you begin to operate from an open heart, you become a clear channel for God's use where you can more easily use your skills and talents to make the world a better place. By the term "better," I mean more harmonious, more inclusive, more cooperative, and more loving.

Rescue Your Inner Child

There is a "way of being" in the world where you can express your full potential without it taking anything away from another. That way of being exists in 5D reality. Unfortunately, in 3D reality there is a fundamental belief in "lack and limitation". This is the crux of the problems we face. This way of being that only results in a zero-sum game in which someone wins, and someone loses. So, most of us believe if "I do for you… I can't do for myself." We must get beyond this limited way of seeing reality.

Our way of being in 3D has us looking at our current reality through the "filters of our past". Many of us claim to need a "frame of reference" to make good decisions. Nothing could be further from the truth. It is this kind of thought process that keeps you chained to your past. Time to let go of your "frame of reference" which was distorted in its original absorption of information. Time to replace that way of being with "divine guidance" where all variables are already accounted for, and the optimal outcome is readily available.

How do we get there? How do we overcome our view of reality through the lenses of lack and limitation? For me, permanent change is made by accessing the root cause of the beliefs. That's why you have so many life coaches forever telling you that you've got to deal with your past. You've got to reconcile it. You've got to transform. To me this really means going internal to rescue your inner child who is stuck, scared, and afraid without the skills to deal with what is happening in their world. As a result, the only ways to cope are often to lash out or withdraw.

The original issues which created your personality are not as important as the willingness to go and retrieve your inner child so that you can become a whole person within yourself. You can't make change in the world that is lasting and permanent, if you are not whole within yourself. There is a process for those of us who have been stuck by trauma and drama of our childhood. There is a process to release this emotional energy. That is what life coaches do. That is what therapists do. That is what psychologists do. That is what pastoral counselors do. There are people available that can help you move through this process helping you identify where you are stuck. It is exceedingly difficult at times to do this by yourself because most of the time you are in a feedback loop of your ego, so you only hear what you want to hear, which reinforces what you already know. To step beyond the ego, it is time to learn to navigate in 5D.

Navigating in 5D

In your spiritual awakening comes added information and skills. You will soon learn your mind has been opened with access to a higher multi-sensory way of navigating in 5D which is better than the antiquated "frame of reference". Many of us already know but don't truly value these traits. Everyone has heard of clairvoyance but are you familiar with the other senses such as clairaudience, clairsentience, or clair-cognizance. In the 5D reality, lots of information is processed simultaneously from several different inputs. Using your multi-sensory way of being allows you to always be "ahead of the game" in your response because you are never surprised by anything that happens. There is an early warning system that you now have access to that does not depend on external verification. You already know that you know.

Clairvoyance (clear seeing): Most of us trust what we see with our own eyes, but some can see things that have not happened yet. We laugh and say that person is "clairvoyant." This ability is amplified in your spiritual awakening where your "third-eye" in the center of your forehead allows your intuitive side to see things in visions or dreams that eventually come to pass. This ability is why many in 3D can't get away with anything because it is already being seen and steps already taken to mitigate the impending impact. Some of you already have this ability, trust it. It will not steer you wrong, trust your clairvoyance.

Clairaudience (clear hearing): Some of you are like me, you are clairaudient, so your ears pick up every little sound. Not only do you hear everything in this dimension but also in the next. You can hear the "still small voice of God." The intuitive directions and divine guidance come as a voice from the Spirit that you can hear very clearly just like someone standing next to you talking. If you trust this information, even if there is no external verification, you will find out later why you were told to do something a certain way. It is always revealed.

Clairsentience (clear feeling): Some of us have lived life with the accusation that "you are just too sensitive." Yes, that is true because we are clairsentient. I sometimes describe this "as living life next to concert speakers." Whenever someone is highly emotional, it is like listening to them in stereo. For me, when people were arguing, not only could I hear it, but I could also physically feel it in the pit of my stomach (solar plexus). If you are clairsentient, learn to trust what you are feeling because your feelings may be related to current events or foreshadowing events to come. Remember, no external verification is needed. All will be revealed in time.

Clair-cognizance (clear knowing): How do you know that? This is the question that people who are clair-cognizant are often asked. People often talk to you and by the time they finish talking, you respond with exactly what they need to hear. The thing is when you're speaking to them, you are also hearing the solutions for the first time yourself. When people talk, you are not analyzing the information being said, it's when they stop talking and you respond that the information automatically flows. In a state of clair-cognizance you don't even know, how you know, yet what you are saying is given from such a place of conviction and confidence. What people need to understand is your being connected to your inner self is what allows this information to be channeled through you, but it is not from you.

All these multi-sensory abilities available in the fifth dimensional reality are here to help you navigate the physical reality. At times, they can give you advanced warning. They can also give you a way to stay in the flow or in the synchronicity of life. The use of and trust in these multi-senses allow you to stay anchored in your centeredness which results in being completely in your joy, fully in your happiness, and harmonious in your peace.

Chapter 16

Time is Up

Many people think being spiritual requires you to "sacrifice yourself" for God. I am not sure where this distorted belief originates because if you look at what God created in nature, you will see nothing but abundance. It is only the ego in humans who have a desire to limit or restrict others. Nowhere in nature does one tree grow and say to another tree, "you need to wait until I finish growing before you can grow" or one blade of grass say to another blade of grass "you need to wait until I die before you can grow." Everything God created gives others room to grow. So, why is it humans don't do that? Humans guided by their ego without hesitation will easily say "You need to help me first then I will help you."

In the stories you just read, unless we dissolve our attachment to our ego, we cannot make room for anyone else's needs or concerns. Time is up for functioning in this manner. It is "time for a new way of being" where each person is given room to grow into their full potential. If you really want to grow, then it is essential you maximize your "spiritual-self" and minimize your "ego-self." As you continue this spiritual journey just remember to be "honest with yourself" which leads to being honest with others. Always trust how you feel, even if there is nothing in your external environment verifying how you feel. In due time, you will see what you need to see to help you make peace with your initial observations.

What Are You Magnetizing?

As was said before, "where attention goes, energy flows," so what are you magnetizing into your experience? How does it reinforce what you believe? Emotions are magnetic, so if you believe the world is full of hateful people then that's what you magnetize. On the contrary, if you believe the world is full of wonderful people then that is what you magnetize. Use your powers wisely, as it is time for a new way of being.

You cannot experience what you don't believe. If you are waiting for your mega millions through the lottery, but you are stuck in your belief about lack and limitation, then sorry, "it isn't going to happen for you"! I'm sure I am not the first writer to say this. We have power to create our lives but the question I'm raising is "Who is leading your creation? Is it your ego-self or your divine- self?

Who Needs Algebra?

I woke up just before the writing of this book with an algebraic equation in my head, "NJ + NA = DG." I thought to myself that looks like an algebraic equation. Who needs algebra? NJ + NA = DG... What does that even mean? Well, I soon found out as I sat for my morning meditation and asked the question. The answer that came back was as follows: "NJ" means non-judgment plus "NA" means non- attachment equals "DG" divine guidance. In short, non-judgement plus non-attachment allows for divine guidance.

Non-judgment goes to the way in which we operate in daily reality. We must find a way to interfere with our ego judging everything we see through the lenses of duality. Everything is being run through the filter of opposites: right/wrong or good/bad. We judge everything despite most of our sacred text admonishing us to "judge not least you be judged."

If we could find a way to connect to our divine self, we would be reminded that we can't judge because there's nothing to judge since nothing has happened to us. Remember, the essential essence of who we are is like steam. Judgement is pointless since there is no need to control or manipulate the material world because the essence of who you are is never really affected?

With regards to non-attachment, if we stop our judgment and criticism, we won't go so quickly into action. As it stands now, when we see what we perceive as a problem, we judge it then go right into action trying to fix it. Breaking the link between judgment and action gives room for divine guidance or the intuitive side of ourselves to step into the decision-making process bringing forward information we have no way of knowing. If you could only pull back your impulse to act, not be so attached to your opinions, you could more clearly see through the divine lenses that what you perceive needs to be done is "not" always what needs to happen.

I Got It Wrong

Since I put my "Ego on Front Street," it seems like the divine guidance I get is the exact opposite of what I feel would be helpful. The things I would normally do, I am being divinely guided not to do while being guided to do things I would "not" normally do. Let me give you an example from my own life.

Recently, my relative put his young children into daycare. To meet the deadline, it required "all hands-on deck." Everybody contributed to buying a variety of things for the children including myself. The weekend before school was to start, we celebrated his son's third birthday at a local restaurant. After the party was over, there was additional shopping that needed to happen. Normally, I would have gone home since I met my commitment to come and have lunch. But being in a relaxed state of mind, I was able to follow divine guidance to continue to hang out and support everyone. I agreed to go to the store to help keep the kids occupied while the adults searched for items on the checklist.

After that I continued to keep the children occupied as I waited for the adults to come back from another store. At that point, I thought I was going to lose my mind when I found out there was still a third store we needed to go to. My relative looked on the verge of exhaustion as she had worked a full-time job that week and went right into babysitting grandchildren. Not an easy task, since everybody knows toddlers can be a handful.

As she was loading the grandchildren into the car, I was guided to offer to do the final shopping errand without her. I told her to "go home" and take the grandchildren and I would bring the final items from the checklist to her. She gave me a big hug as she said, "Oh my God that would be so great."

Now what is interesting about this is normally I would not have taken this additional step. I would have stopped agreeing to spend any more money since I had already shopped for them, bought birthday presents and spent money on lunch. But following my divine guidance, I did the additional shopping without her. When I returned with the requested items, my relative was very appreciative. I share this story to say that we don't always know what needs to be done in situations. We must allow for the fact that we can be wrong. Sometimes, we cannot anticipate all the variables in advance. But trusting in divine guidance allows us to make decisions that are best for everyone.

Being Taken Care of

It's ironic but my biggest fear in life has always been trusting others to look after my best interest. This made it exceedingly difficult at first to learn to trust God. I had to grow into the "Divine Partnership" little by little. I spent much of my spiritual life doing things "for God" but not doing things "with God." So, I often ended up following some of the intuitive impulses while ignoring others. Overtime, I could see that everything my Spirit was guiding me to do was for my own best interest. For the first time, I felt like my interests were being considered and I was truly being taken care of.

Because my theme park revolved around "I don't matter," it took longer to surrender my personal agenda to the divine will. To my delight, now every time I am being given solutions, they always have a beneficial effect on me. For too many of us on a spiritual path, we think surrendering our personal agenda to God's will involves the loss of our individuality. We might also think that if we surrender, we will have to endure endless "self-sacrifice." Nothing could be further from the truth. Stop holding back that small part of yourself that would allow you to fully merge with God.

In this reunification with the Spirit that created you, nothing but perfection comes as the filters through which you see reality become more transparent. As those filters become more transparent, it becomes easier to let go of "ego guidance." The decisions we are divinely guided to make become more harmonious and optimal because these decisions consider more variables including the impact on everyone. Imagine the kind of world we could have if we all anchored this new way of being.

Fears Unfounded

We have a choice as to rather we follow our ego-self or follow our spiritual-self. I have lived most of my life following my ego-self so I know the limitations that following my ego can have. I must pause to express a profound appreciation for my ego as it fought back and fought off others who would try to use and abuse me. I was operating from the belief as one writer put it, "the human ungoverned is more vicious than an animal in the jungle." However, I have reached a point in life where I no longer have the energy that is required to be in constant confrontations that living under ego guidance requires. I am also convinced the "real me" is like "steam" so no matter what happens to my body or possessions, I am unassailable and invulnerable.

Given that I have been blessed to live by the Spirit, I can honestly say I prefer that. All my fears were unfounded in the belief that earthly pleasures would be taken from me, and I would have to endure endless self-sacrifice. That was truer under the direction of my ego. I endured endless self-sacrifice which became the fuel for anger upon which my ego thrived. Therefore, I am choosing to be led by the divine self willingly strengthening my partnership with God. Operating from a place of non-judgment and non-attachment keeps my stress levels down while allowing for divine impulses to help address whatever is before me.

Trust God

It's time for us to do things differently. How do we trust God? In the new way of being, it means allowing your intuitive decisions to come through your heart space. Decisions made from that place are always optimal and inclusive. But many of us who are religious are straddling the fence between "surrendering to God" or "telling God what needs to happen." It is easy to see the challenge in truly giving up our personal agenda. But if we would just trust God in partnership, we could access the higher realms where the information available is beyond our five senses. Can you see the new world with the next level communications where clairvoyance, clairsentience, clairaudience, and clair-cognizance are the norm? Imagine having the ability to make decisions that include variables that you have no way of knowing right now. If you trust in divine guidance, that option is already yours.

The reason this next level decision-making is important is because the outcome will have to be beneficial to the whole. There comes a point on the spiritual journey where it's not easy to make decisions that only benefit you for that way of being no longer brings happiness. What really brings joy is when decisions are made that benefit you but also have a far-reaching positive benefit on others.

What also brings joy is to see each person fulfill their God-given potential to excel in whatever they are good at. It can only benefit the whole to have everyone fulfilling their spiritual destiny. Some people are natural teachers. Some people are natural athletes. Some people are natural musicians. Some people are natural politicians. Some people are natural managers and entrepreneurs. Imagine what the world would look like under divine guidance if we all brought our talents into positive co-creation. There is nothing we could not do together as one global family in partnership with the divine. We could change our systems, structures, and institutions to benefit the whole of humanity. This is what is on the horizon, the question is, "Will you move towards your divine destiny before time is up"?

Afterword
By Kennesha Forrest
Consultant & Entrepreneur – Los Angeles, CA

"What's your contribution to the chaos?" That direct question Robin introduced in the book is the exact question she asked me in one of our many coaching sessions. It hit me like the proverbial "ton of bricks" because my ego was not ready to hear that. "Who me? I do not have a contribution, it's THEM!" "Ego-Me" immediately wanted to offer as a rebuttal, but "Spiritual-Me" knew better. By this point, I had already developed such a relationship with Robin that she knew I was ready to deal with the impact of the question and, more importantly, the answer.

You see, our relationship began back in 2008 when I was at the apex of the demise of my marriage and my family was falling apart. Spirit guided me to Robin, by way of Debbie Ford, and just as the saying goes…" when the student is ready, the teacher appears!" She has since coached me right through the dissolution of my marriage and the journey of putting my kids' and my life back together. Along the way, and soon after, our coach-client relationship acquiesced into a deep friendship that is still going strong.

What I can tell you is that I had a front row seat to view her journey, just as much as she had to mine. I've been right there as she navigated through situations with her loved ones highlighted in her story. I saw how her message transcended from being just "words" into a living, breathing, way of being!

In this book, she is not just writing a story to demonstrate a philosophy. She made way and allowed Spirit to pen the experience through her and get right to the heart of the matter—shedding light on how the Ego runs our lives sometimes, especially when we think we are so "spiritual."

Witnessing her journey and being a listening ear along the way has allowed me to "level up" and give proper place to my ego as well; even when I sometimes do so while pouting and folding my arms in protest like a little girl having a tantrum.

Robin taught me that it is "Ok" to have emotional expression. To be "pissed- off" is just as much a part of the human experience as expressing sadness, frustration, love, joy, happiness, and desire! To deny ourselves the space and permission to fully express our human emotions is an afront to the divinity in each of us. We chose this human experience (whether we agree or not) and to deem any part of it "wrong," is to say that Divine Intelligence, God, Spirit, Source (whatever you choose to call it) made a mistake; this is impossible, no matter how it looks. Living in these "Earth Suits" comes with a lot of "stuff;" a whole gambit of possibilities that will evoke a myriad of choices of expression.

We get stuck when we will not accept this and when we try to stifle or "pray it away." Robin and I agreed that that is a big one for humanity, that religious piece. As a PK (preacher's kid) raised in a strict Christian Pentecostal household in addition to the minefields that are the Black and Female experiences, any expression other than joy, glee, contentment, etc., is often frowned upon or, dare I say, feared. It makes people uncomfortable, and we are not even comfortable ourselves. This is highlighted even more if such expression is in any way in opposition to what is expected. Not expressing is harmful; harmful to our bodies, our minds, and our spirits, no matter how we choose to present in our human bodies. This unexpressed emotionality (Robin taught me that, too) is where the ego can truly blossom and gains moment to run the show of our lives.

I think it is beyond time for Robin's message to come forth, as she declared in the section titled TRUST GOD (pg. 120). If the events and state of the world over the last few years have shown us anything (especially post-COVID), it is that humanity must do something different to sustain and survive in a healthy way. Survival and the ability to thrive going forward will require us to be "heart-centered" and fully authentic. I'm so grateful to be able to witness Robin getting this message out to the world.

Why do I believe it will *"now"* be well received as opposed to before? I believe this because "clear channels" like Robin have lived what they are bringing forth (I love that term that she coined and shared with me one day). It must happen this way, as humanity cannot afford more convoluted messengers leading with ego dressed in spiritual clothes. Robin is among the Light-Bringers, showing us what it looks like to be "in partnership with the Divine." True Harmony simply will not happen without this partnership. I'm so thankful to be along for the ride. What a wonderful time to be alive!

Suggested Readings

Braden, Gregg, *The Spontaneous Healing of Belief*, Hay House Inc., New York, NY

Chapman, Gary, *The 5 Love Languages: The Secret to Love That Lasts*, Northfield Publishing, Chicago

Dyer, Wayne, Ph.D., *There's a Spiritual Solution to Every Problem*, HarperCollins, New York, NY

Dyer, Wayne, Ph.D., *Change Your Thoughts-Change Your Life*, Hay House Inc., New York, NY

Dyer, Wayne, Ph.D., *Excuses Begone! How to Change Lifelong, Self-Defeating Thinking Habits*, Hay House Inc., New York, NY

Ford, Debbie, *Courage: Igniting Self Confidence*, HarperCollins, New York, NY

Ford, Debbie, *The 21-Day Consciousness Cleanse: A Breakthrough Program for Connecting with Your Soul's Deepest Purpose*, HarperCollins, New York

Ford, Debbie, *The Dark Side of the Light Chasers*, Riverhead Books (Division of Penguin Putnam) New York, NY

Foundation for Inner Peace, *A Course in Miracles, Combined Volume-Third Edition*, Foundation for Inner Peace, Mill Valley, CA

Fox, Emmet, *The Sermon on the Mount: The Key to Success in Life*, HarperCollins, San Francisco, CA

Goldsmith, Joel, *The Thunder of Silence*, HarperCollins, San Francisco, CA

Goldsmith, Joel, *Practicing the Presence: The Inspirational Guide to Regaining Meaning and a Sense of Purpose in Life*, HarperCollins, San Francisco, CA

Hay, Louise, *You Can Heal Your Life*, Hay House Inc., Carlsbad, CA

Hicks, Esther and Jerry, *Ask and It Is Given: Learning to Manifest Your Desires*, Hay House, Carlsbad, CA

Jakes, T.D., *Instinct: The Power to Unleash Your Inborn Drive*, Faith Words (Hachette Book Group), New York, NY

Johnson, Robin L., *Awakening of a Chocolate Mystic*, Balboa Press (Division of Hay House), Bloomington, IN

Johnson, Robin L., *ETA 2 Oneness: A Journey to Spiritual Awakening*, Balboa Press (Division of Hay House), Bloomington, IN

Krishna, Manoj, *Understanding Me, Understanding You – An Enquiry into Being Human,* Cleartree Press, London, England

Krishna, Manoj, *Stress Free – Understand Yourself, Discover Wisdom, Be Free,* Cleartree Press, London, England

Meyer, Joyce, *Battlefield of the Mind: Winning the Battlefield in Your Mind*, Warner Books Inc., New York, NY

Meyer, Joyce, *Change Your Words Change Your Life: Understanding the Power of Every Word You Speak*, Faith Words (Hachette Book Group), New York, NY

Moses, Jeffrey, *Oneness: Great Principles Shared by All Religions*, Ballantine Books, New York, NY

Osteen, Joel, *Break Out: 5 Keys to Go Beyond Your Barriers and Live and Extraordinary Life*, Faith Words (Hachette Book Group), New York, NY

Tolle, Eckhart, *A New Earth: Awakening to Your Life's Purpose*, Button (Penguin Group), New York, NY

Vanzant, Iyanla, *Peace from Broken Pieces: How to Get Through What You're Going Through*, Hay House Inc., New York, NY

About the Author

 Ms. Robin L. Johnson is a Spiritual Transformation Coach and Executive Director of the ETA 2 Oneness Institute, an organization that supports people in their spiritual awakening. By using life coaching techniques, people can operate on a higher level of consciousness by learning to minimize their ego driven behaviors while maximizing their divine decision-making.

Ms. Johnson has always tried to find answers to some of life's most pressing questions such as "Is it really possible to practice tolerance, patience, kindness and love in a world full of violence, anger, hatred and selfishness?" She sought answers through the study of the world's major religious traditions including Christianity, Judaism, Islam, Taoism, Hinduism, and Buddhism.

Ms. Johnson integrated her study of religious traditions with travel to forty countries around the world where these religious traditions are practiced including: Italy, Israel, Egypt, China, India, Thailand, and Peru. After studying personal and spiritual development as a hobby for 20 years while working as a management consultant, Ms. Johnson finally opened her own institute to share her concepts.

Having achieved her version of the "American Dream," Ms. Johnson became more dissatisfied as she felt separated and isolated from God. One day after seeing Debbie Ford, New York Times Bestselling Author on Oprah talking about the "shadow beliefs," Ms. Johnson soon realized what was missing from her life. It was access to her own emotionality which had been tied up with past trauma.

Afraid to fully express for fear of what would emerge, she hunkered down in trying to reach God through her mind. As Debbie Ford was fond of saying, the "longest journey you will ever take is the one from your head to your heart." Ms. Johnson became a certified life coach under Debbie Ford.

Ms. Johnson values education, so in addition to obtaining a Certificate in Life Coaching, she has obtained the following: BA, MA, MBA, and Certificate in Christian Ministry. Currently, Ms. Johnson who resides in suburban Philadelphia is a speaker, author, and spiritual transformation coach.

www.eta2oneness.com

Printed in the United States
by Baker & Taylor Publisher Services